#47-0102 Ungummed   #47-0103 Pre-Gummed

WD

It's all yours, Snoopy

Selected Cartoons from
You've Come a Long Way, Charlie Brown; Vol. 1

by CHARLES M. SCHULZ

FAWCETT CREST • NEW YORK

A Fawcett Crest Book
Published by Ballantine Books
Contents of Book: PEANUTS® comic strips by Charles M. Schulz
 Published in the United States by Ballantine Books, a division of Random House, Inc., New York, and simultaneously in Canada by Random House of Canada Limited, Toronto.

ISBN 0-449-20963-4

This edition published by arrangement with Holt, Rinehart and Winston, Inc.

Printed in Canada

First Fawcett Crest Edition: November 1975
First Ballantine Books Edition: April 1983
Second Printing: July 1985

It's All Yours, Snoopy

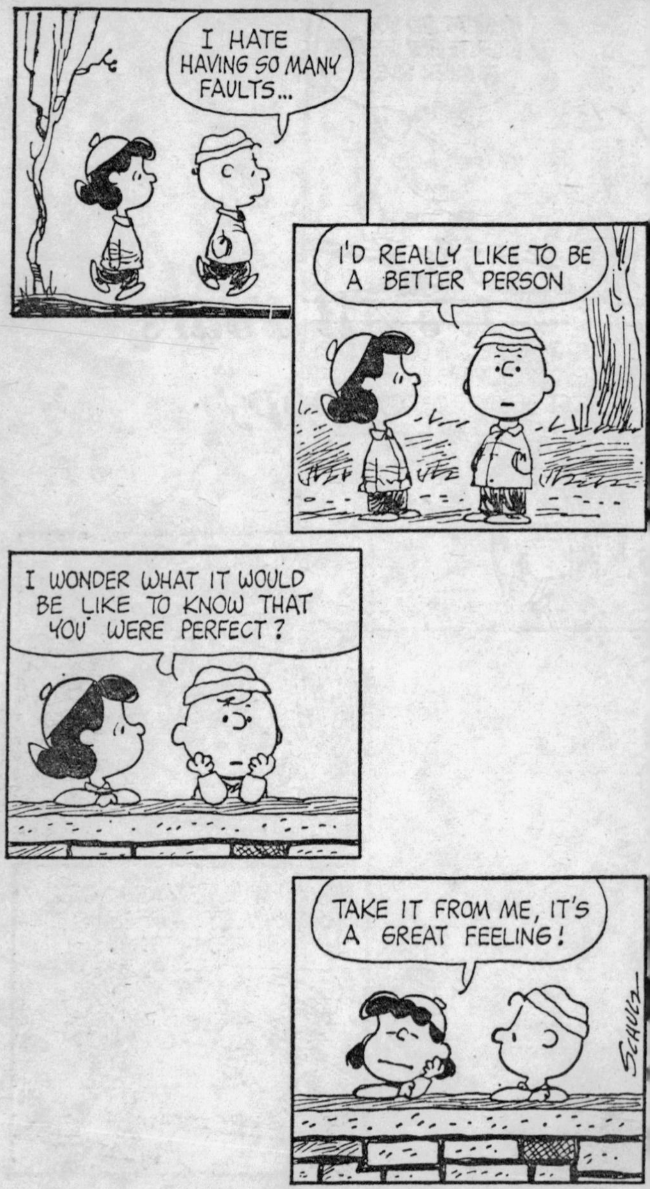
I HATE HAVING SO MANY FAULTS...
I'D REALLY LIKE TO BE A BETTER PERSON
I WONDER WHAT IT WOULD BE LIKE TO KNOW THAT YOU WERE PERFECT?
TAKE IT FROM ME, IT'S A GREAT FEELING!
SCHULZ

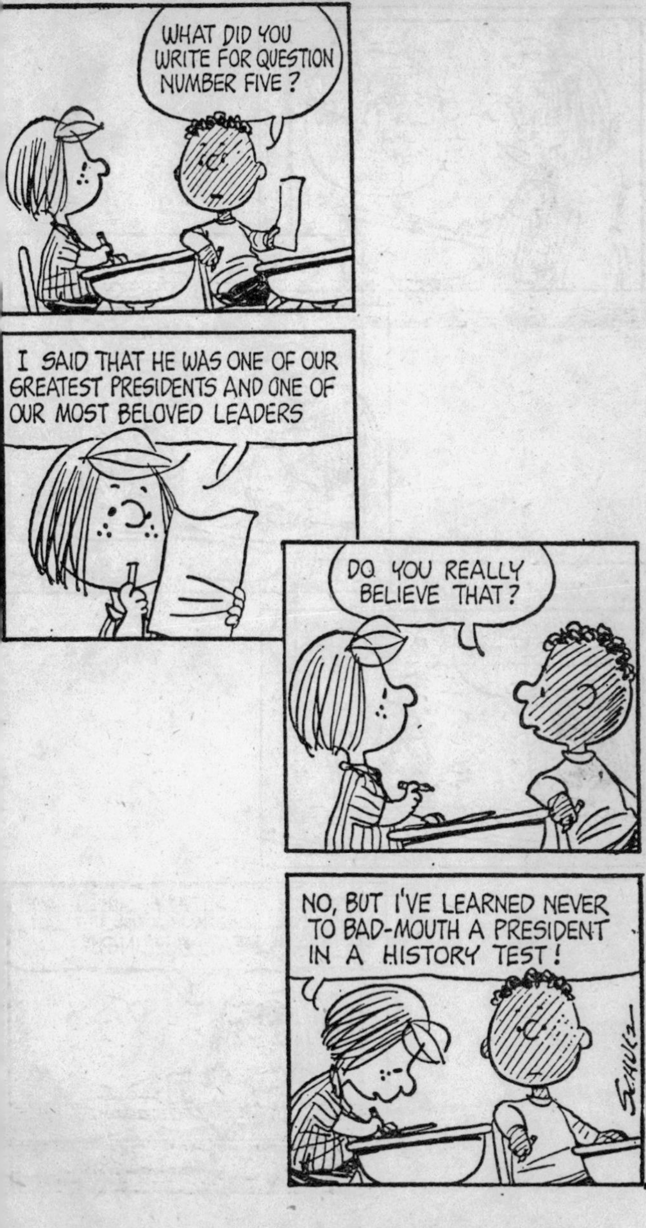
WHAT DID YOU WRITE FOR QUESTION NUMBER FIVE?
I SAID THAT HE WAS ONE OF OUR GREATEST PRESIDENTS AND ONE OF OUR MOST BELOVED LEADERS
DO YOU REALLY BELIEVE THAT?
NO, BUT I'VE LEARNED NEVER TO BAD-MOUTH A PRESIDENT IN A HISTORY TEST!
SCHULZ

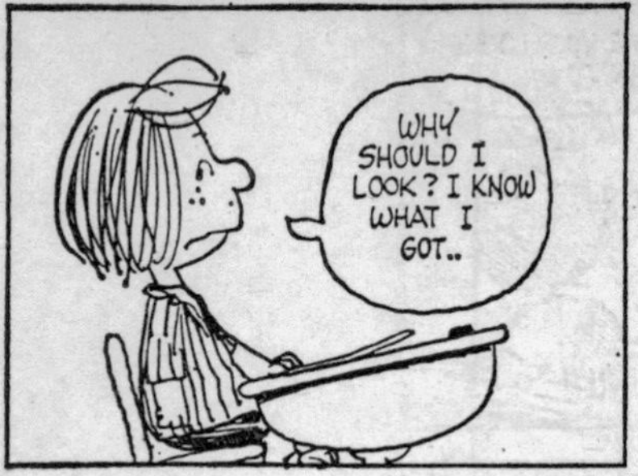
WHY SHOULD I LOOK? I KNOW WHAT I GOT..

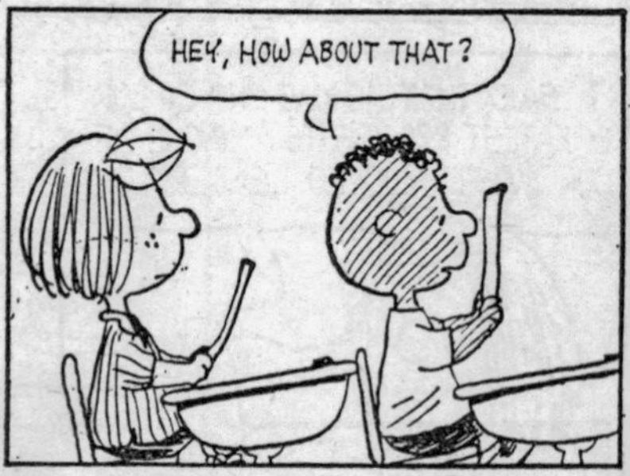
HEY, HOW ABOUT THAT?

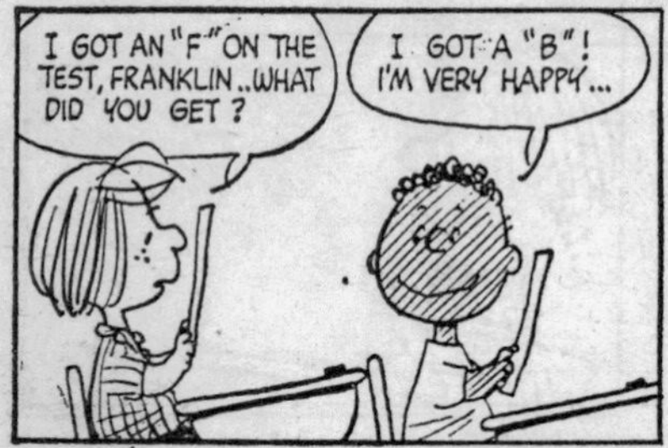
I GOT AN "F" ON THE TEST, FRANKLIN..WHAT DID YOU GET?
I GOT A "B"! I'M VERY HAPPY...

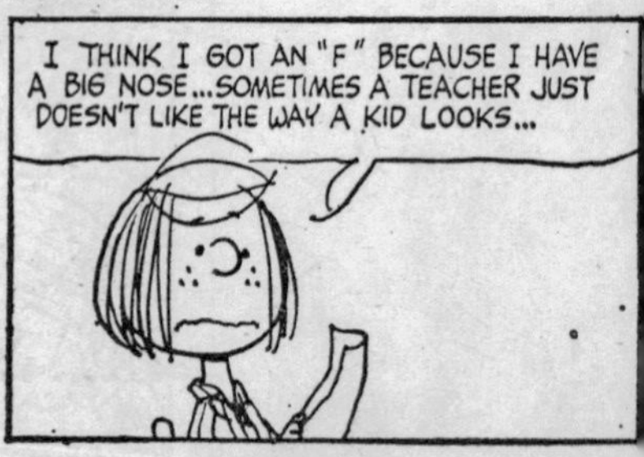
I THINK I GOT AN "F" BECAUSE I HAVE A BIG NOSE...SOMETIMES A TEACHER JUST DOESN'T LIKE THE WAY A KID LOOKS...

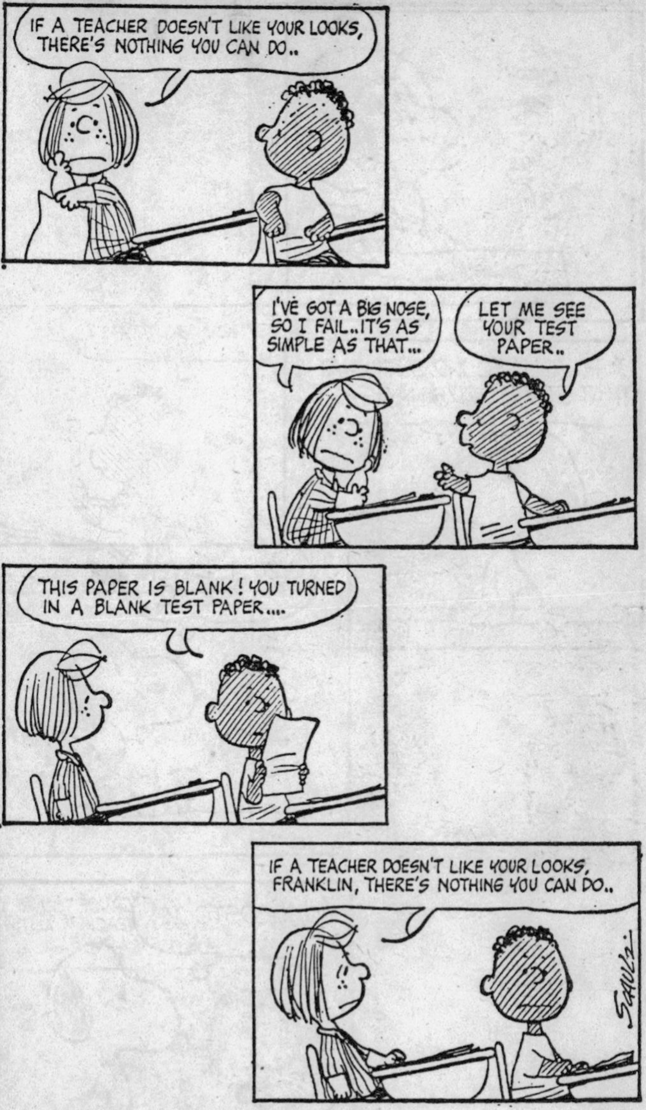
IF A TEACHER DOESN'T LIKE YOUR LOOKS, THERE'S NOTHING YOU CAN DO..
I'VE GOT A BIG NOSE, SO I FAIL..IT'S AS SIMPLE AS THAT...
LET ME SEE YOUR TEST PAPER..
THIS PAPER IS BLANK! YOU TURNED IN A BLANK TEST PAPER....
IF A TEACHER DOESN'T LIKE YOUR LOOKS, FRANKLIN, THERE'S NOTHING YOU CAN DO..
SCHULZ

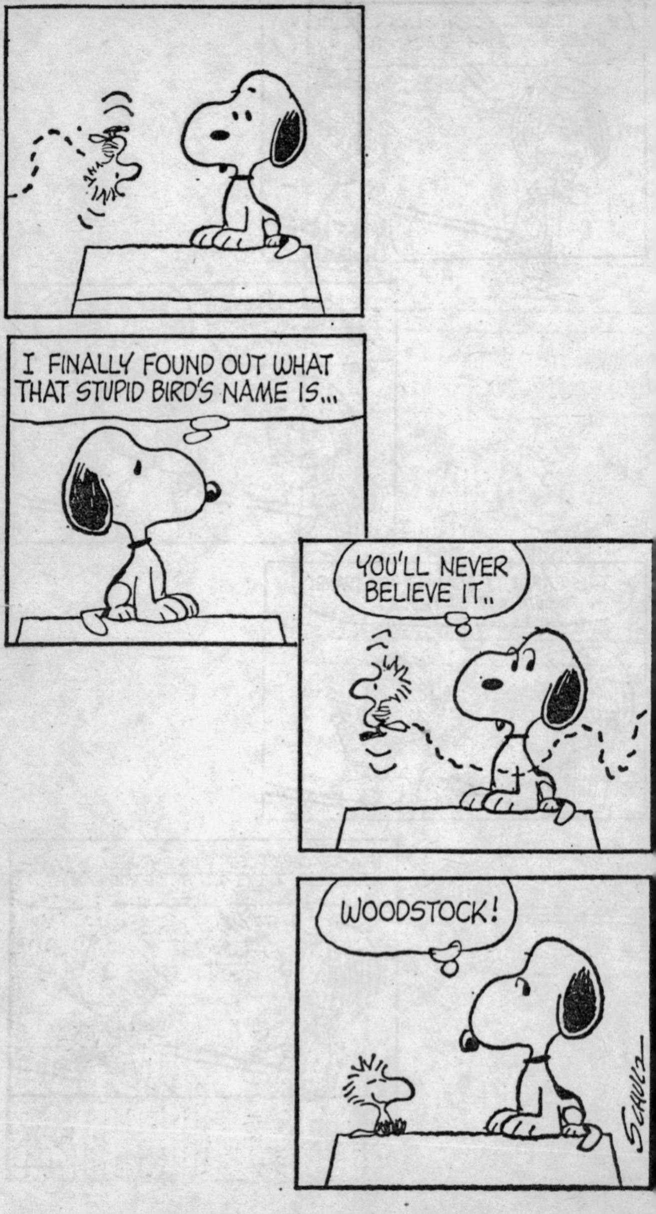
I FINALLY FOUND OUT WHAT THAT STUPID BIRD'S NAME IS...
YOU'LL NEVER BELIEVE IT..
WOODSTOCK!
SCHULZ

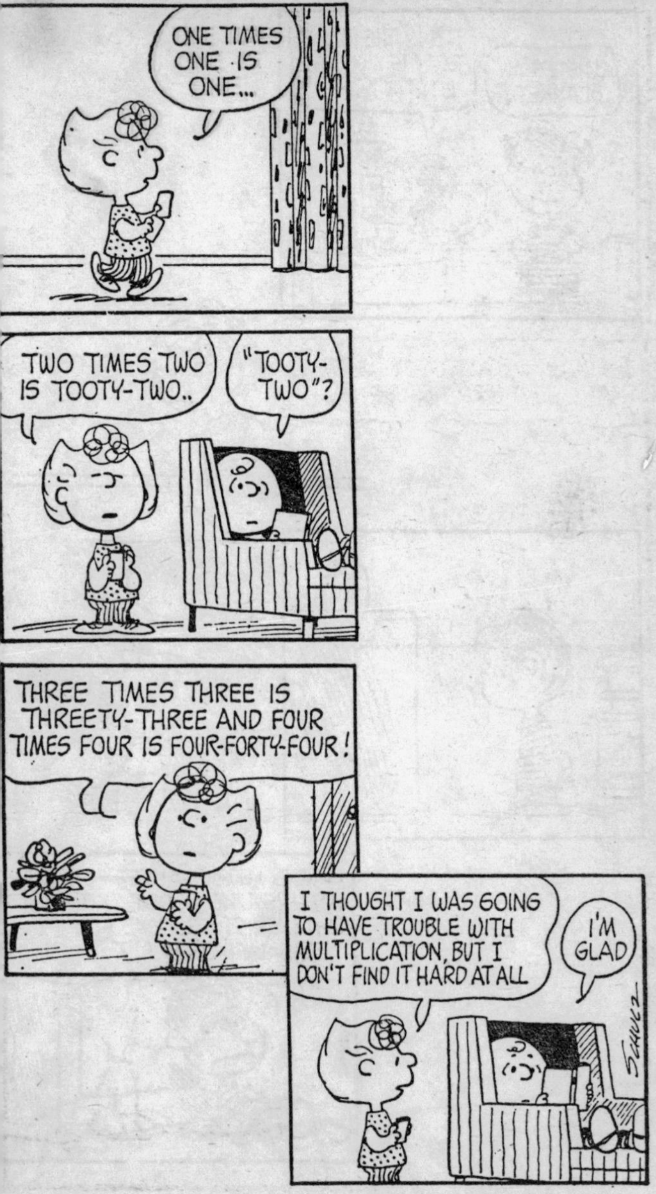
ONE TIMES ONE IS ONE...
TWO TIMES TWO IS TOOTY-TWO..
"TOOTY-TWO"?
THREE TIMES THREE IS THREETY-THREE AND FOUR TIMES FOUR IS FOUR-FORTY-FOUR!
I THOUGHT I WAS GOING TO HAVE TROUBLE WITH MULTIPLICATION, BUT I DON'T FIND IT HARD AT ALL
I'M GLAD
SCHULZ

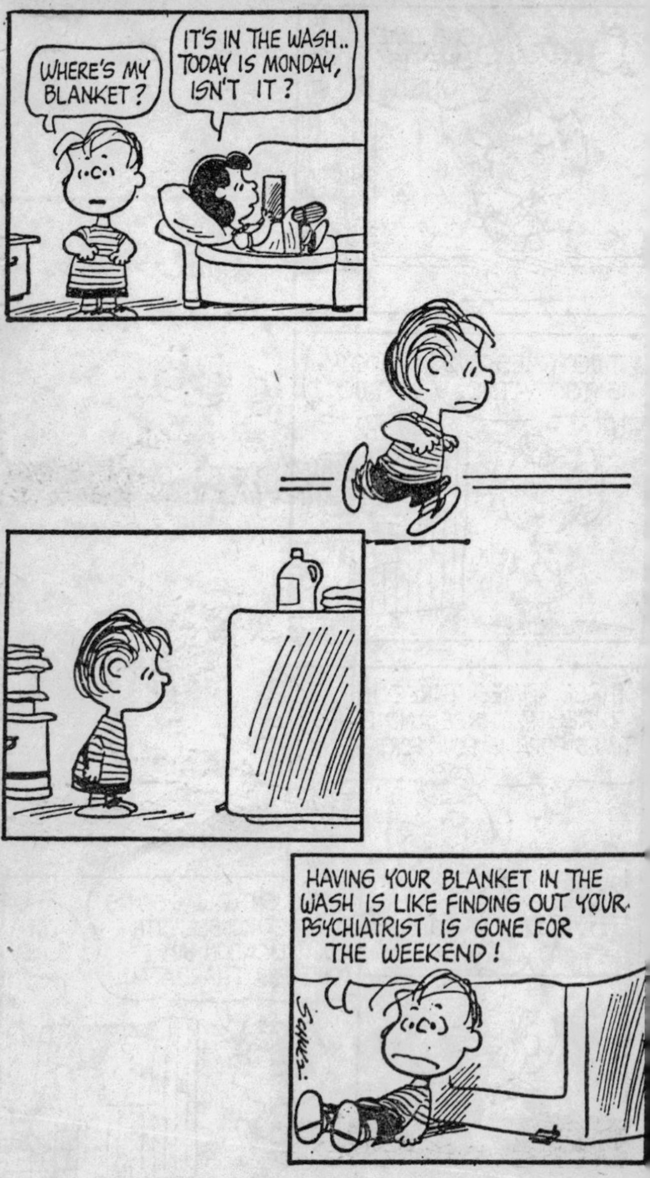
WHERE'S MY BLANKET?
IT'S IN THE WASH.. TODAY IS MONDAY, ISN'T IT?
HAVING YOUR BLANKET IN THE WASH IS LIKE FINDING OUT YOUR PSYCHIATRIST IS GONE FOR THE WEEKEND!
SCHULZ

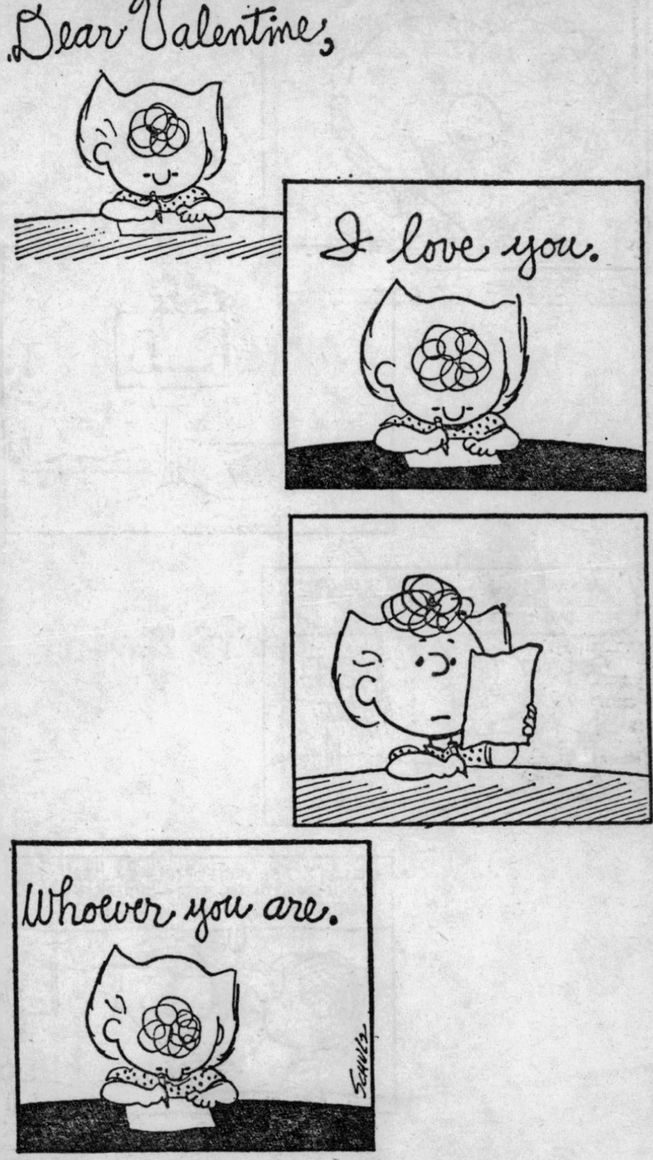
Dear Valentine,
I love you.
Whoever you are.
SCHULZ

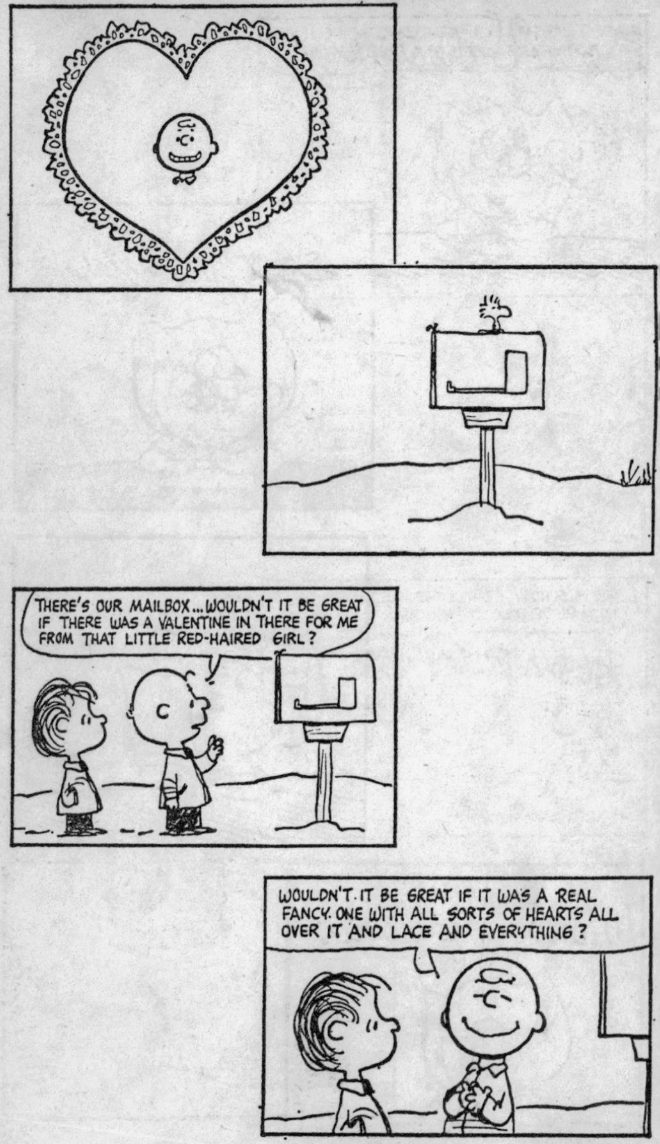
THERE'S OUR MAILBOX...WOULDN'T IT BE GREAT IF THERE WAS A VALENTINE IN THERE FOR ME FROM THAT LITTLE RED-HAIRED GIRL?
WOULDN'T IT BE GREAT IF IT WAS A REAL FANCY ONE WITH ALL SORTS OF HEARTS ALL OVER IT AND LACE AND EVERYTHING?

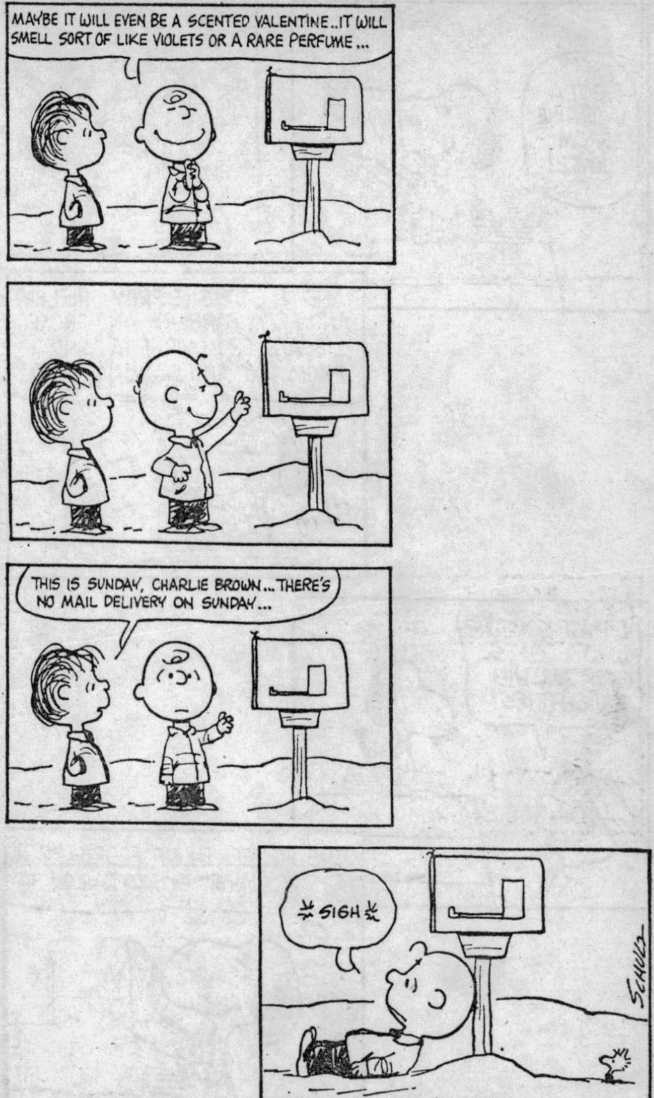
MAYBE IT WILL EVEN BE A SCENTED VALENTINE..IT WILL SMELL SORT OF LIKE VIOLETS OR A RARE PERFUME...
THIS IS SUNDAY, CHARLIE BROWN...THERE'S NO MAIL DELIVERY ON SUNDAY...
SIGH
SCHULZ

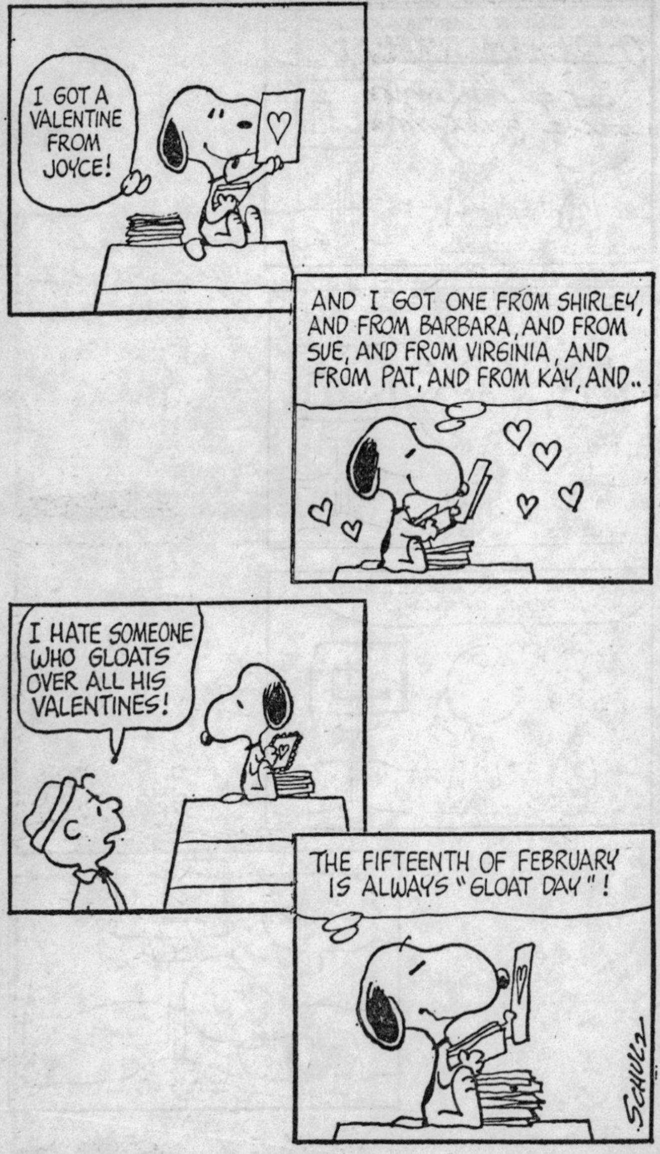
I GOT A VALENTINE FROM JOYCE!
AND I GOT ONE FROM SHIRLEY, AND FROM BARBARA, AND FROM SUE, AND FROM VIRGINIA, AND FROM PAT, AND FROM KAY, AND..
I HATE SOMEONE WHO GLOATS OVER ALL HIS VALENTINES!
THE FIFTEENTH OF FEBRUARY IS ALWAYS "GLOAT DAY"!
SCHULZ

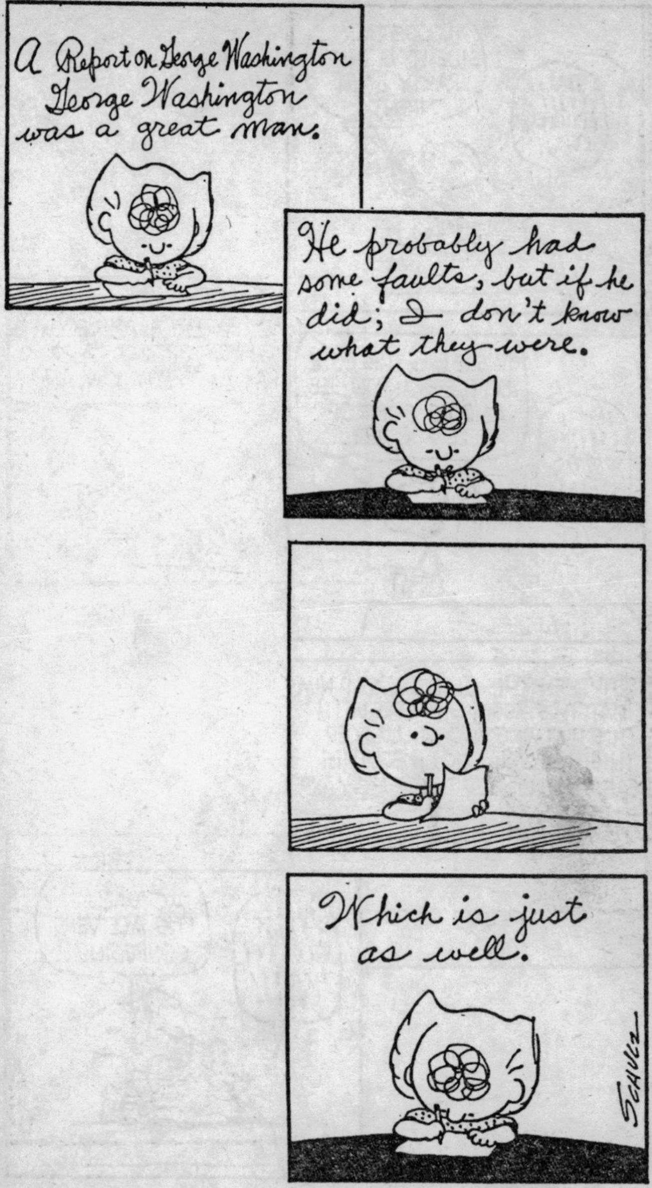
A Report on George Washington
George Washington was a great man.
He probably had some faults, but if he did; I don't know what they were.
Which is just as well.
SCHULZ

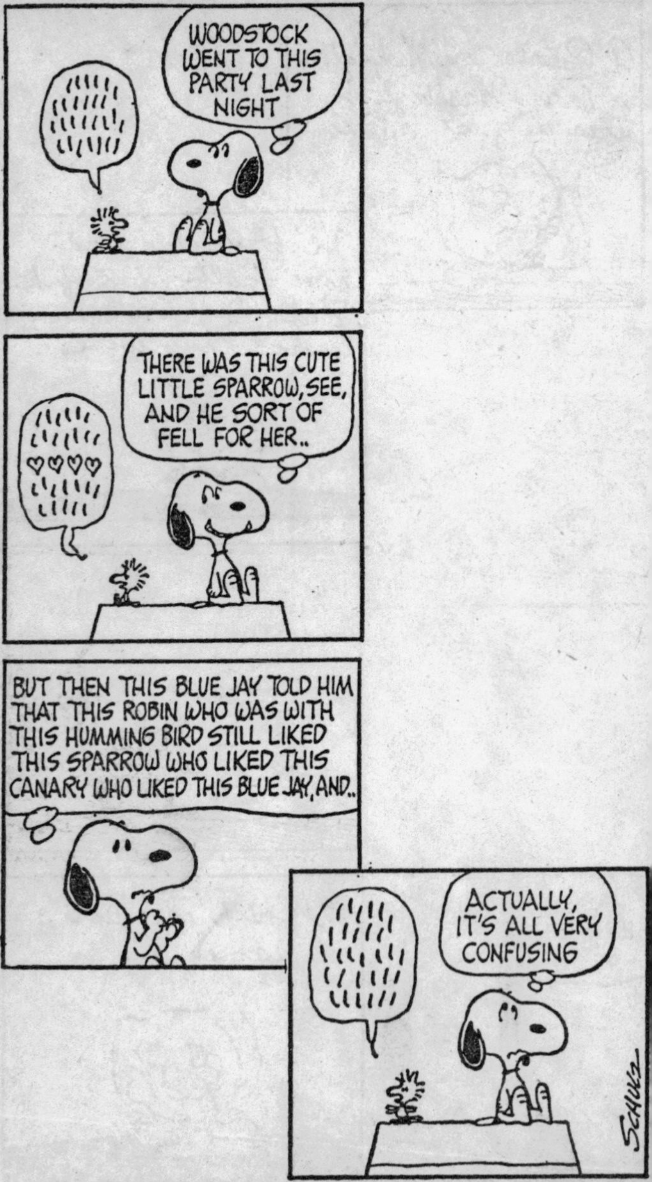
WOODSTOCK WENT TO THIS PARTY LAST NIGHT
THERE WAS THIS CUTE LITTLE SPARROW, SEE, AND HE SORT OF FELL FOR HER..
BUT THEN THIS BLUE JAY TOLD HIM THAT THIS ROBIN WHO WAS WITH THIS HUMMING BIRD STILL LIKED THIS SPARROW WHO LIKED THIS CANARY WHO LIKED THIS BLUE JAY, AND..
ACTUALLY, IT'S ALL VERY CONFUSING
SCHULZ

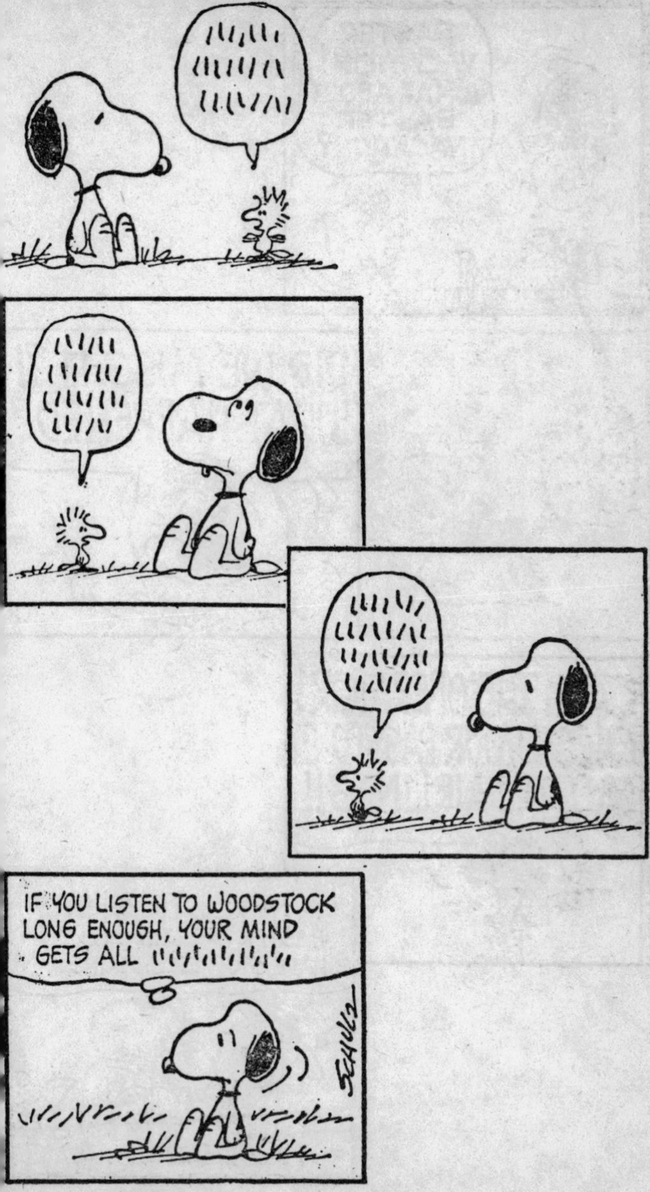
IF YOU LISTEN TO WOODSTOCK LONG ENOUGH, YOUR MIND GETS ALL
SCHULZ

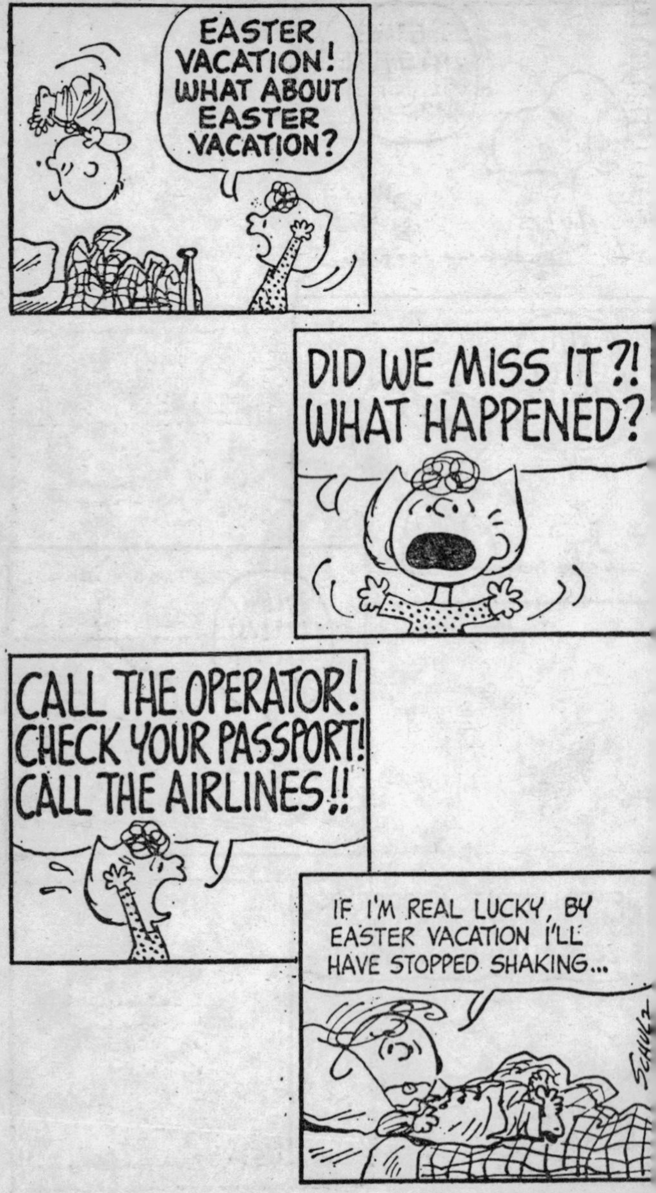
EASTER VACATION! WHAT ABOUT EASTER VACATION?
DID WE MISS IT?! WHAT HAPPENED?
CALL THE OPERATOR! CHECK YOUR PASSPORT! CALL THE AIRLINES!!
IF I'M REAL LUCKY, BY EASTER VACATION I'LL HAVE STOPPED SHAKING...
SCHULZ

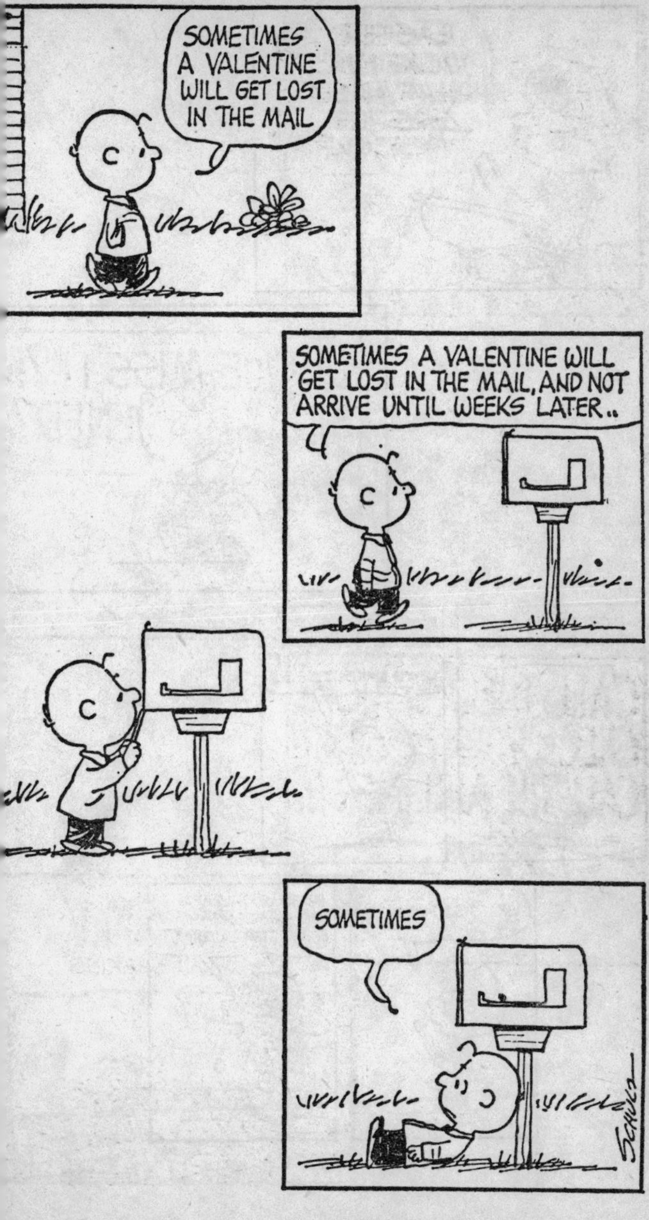
SOMETIMES A VALENTINE WILL GET LOST IN THE MAIL
SOMETIMES A VALENTINE WILL GET LOST IN THE MAIL, AND NOT ARRIVE UNTIL WEEKS LATER..
SOMETIMES
SCHULZ

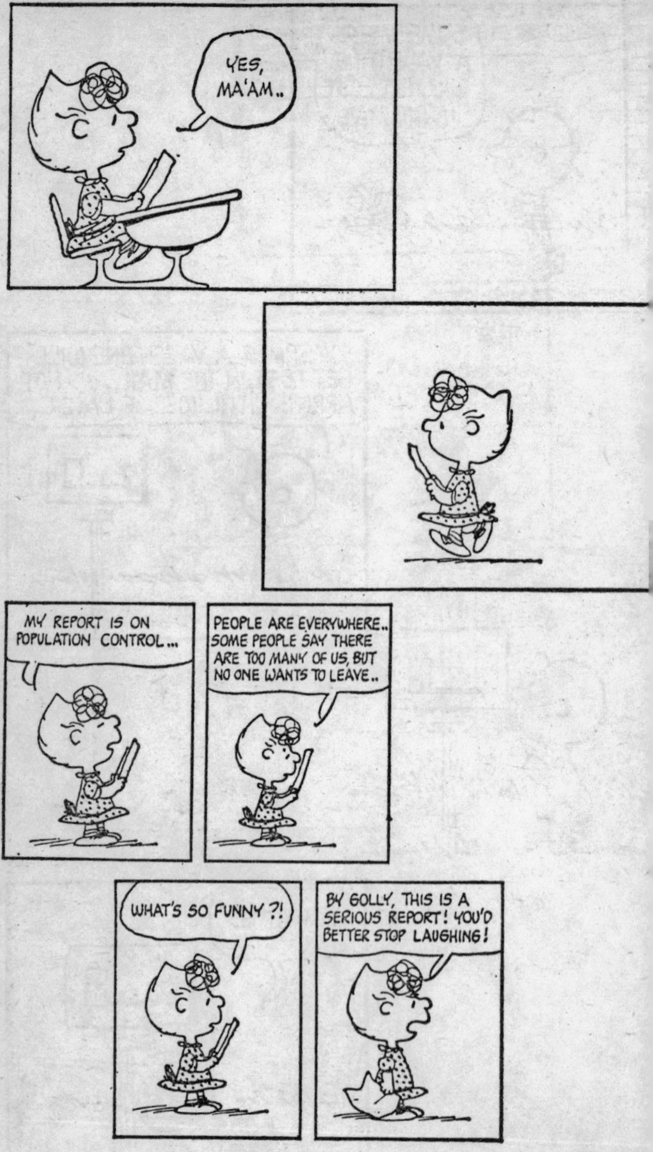
YES, MA'AM..
MY REPORT IS ON POPULATION CONTROL...
PEOPLE ARE EVERYWHERE.. SOME PEOPLE SAY THERE ARE TOO MANY OF US, BUT NO ONE WANTS TO LEAVE..
WHAT'S SO FUNNY ?!
BY GOLLY, THIS IS A SERIOUS REPORT! YOU'D BETTER STOP LAUGHING!

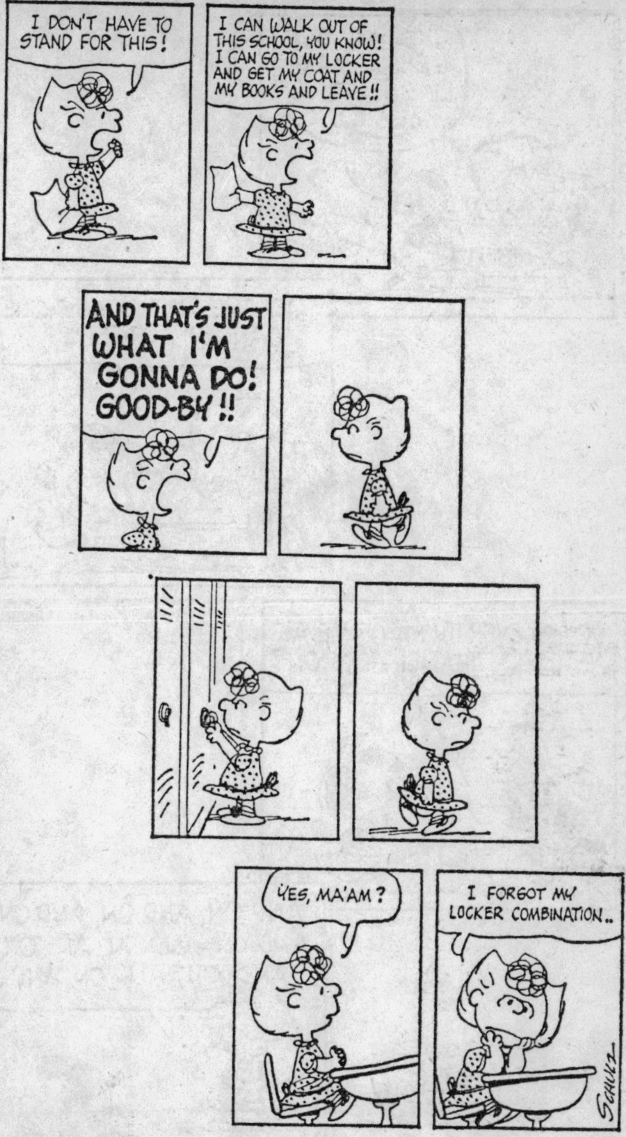
I DON'T HAVE TO STAND FOR THIS!
I CAN WALK OUT OF THIS SCHOOL, YOU KNOW! I CAN GO TO MY LOCKER AND GET MY COAT AND MY BOOKS AND LEAVE!!
AND THAT'S JUST WHAT I'M GONNA DO! GOOD-BY!!
YES, MA'AM?
I FORGOT MY LOCKER COMBINATION..
SCHULZ

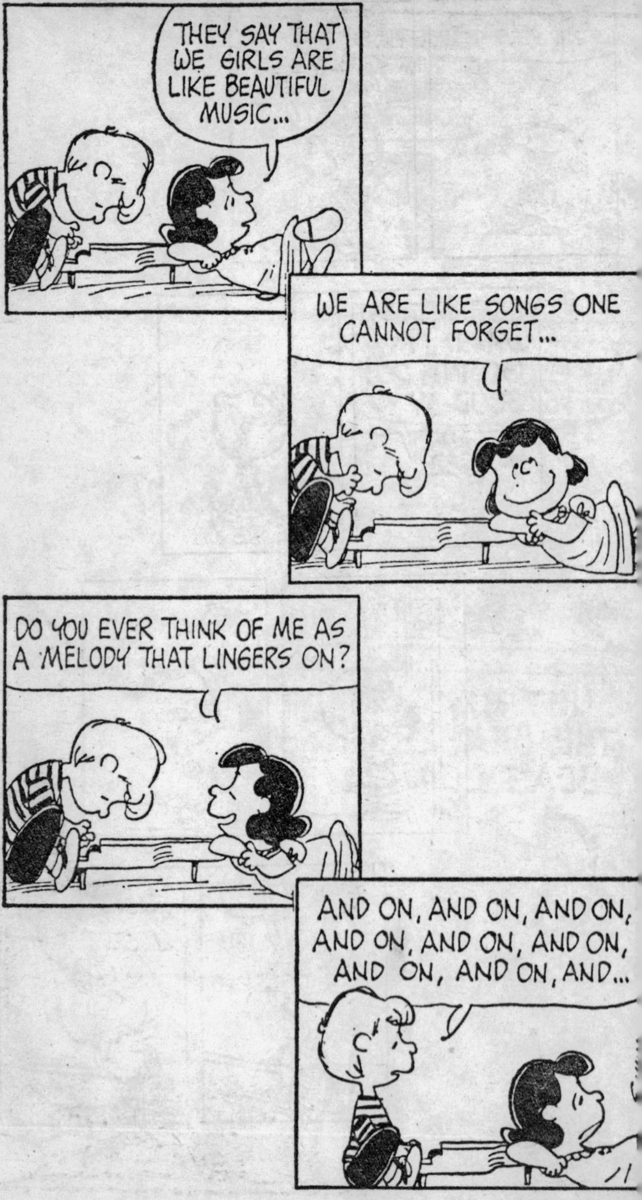
THEY SAY THAT WE GIRLS ARE LIKE BEAUTIFUL MUSIC...
WE ARE LIKE SONGS ONE CANNOT FORGET...
DO YOU EVER THINK OF ME AS A MELODY THAT LINGERS ON?
AND ON, AND ON, AND ON, AND ON, AND ON, AND ON, AND ON, AND ON, AND ON, AND...

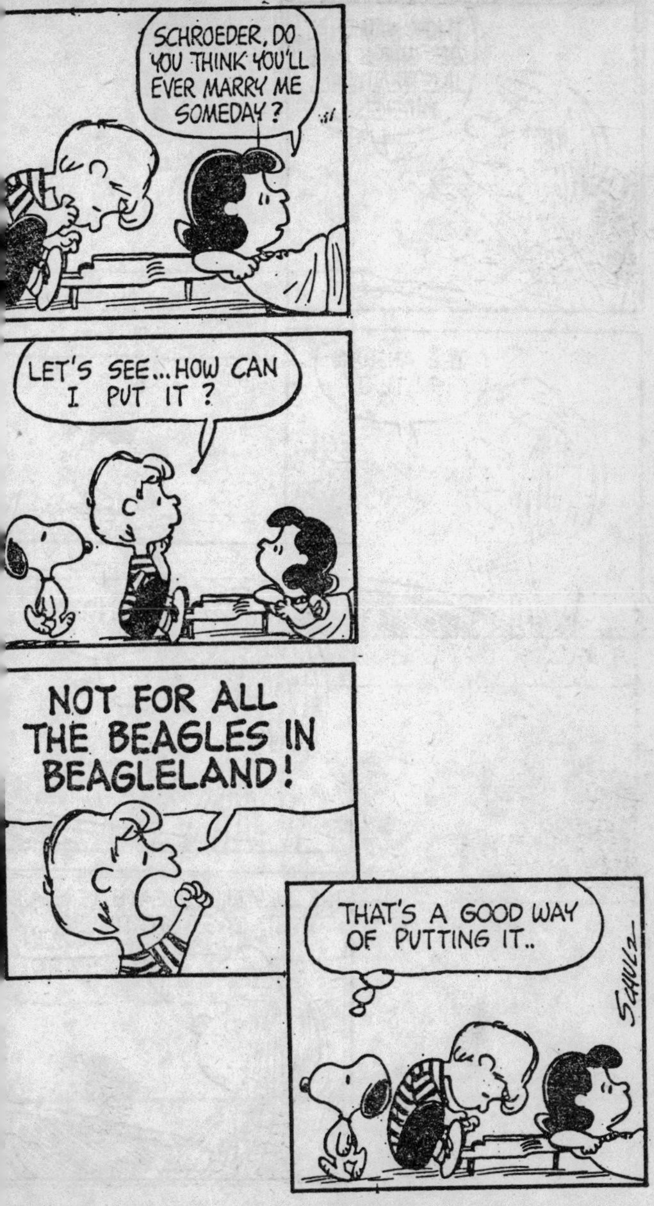
SCHROEDER, DO YOU THINK YOU'LL EVER MARRY ME SOMEDAY?
LET'S SEE...HOW CAN I PUT IT?
NOT FOR ALL THE BEAGLES IN BEAGLELAND!
THAT'S A GOOD WAY OF PUTTING IT..

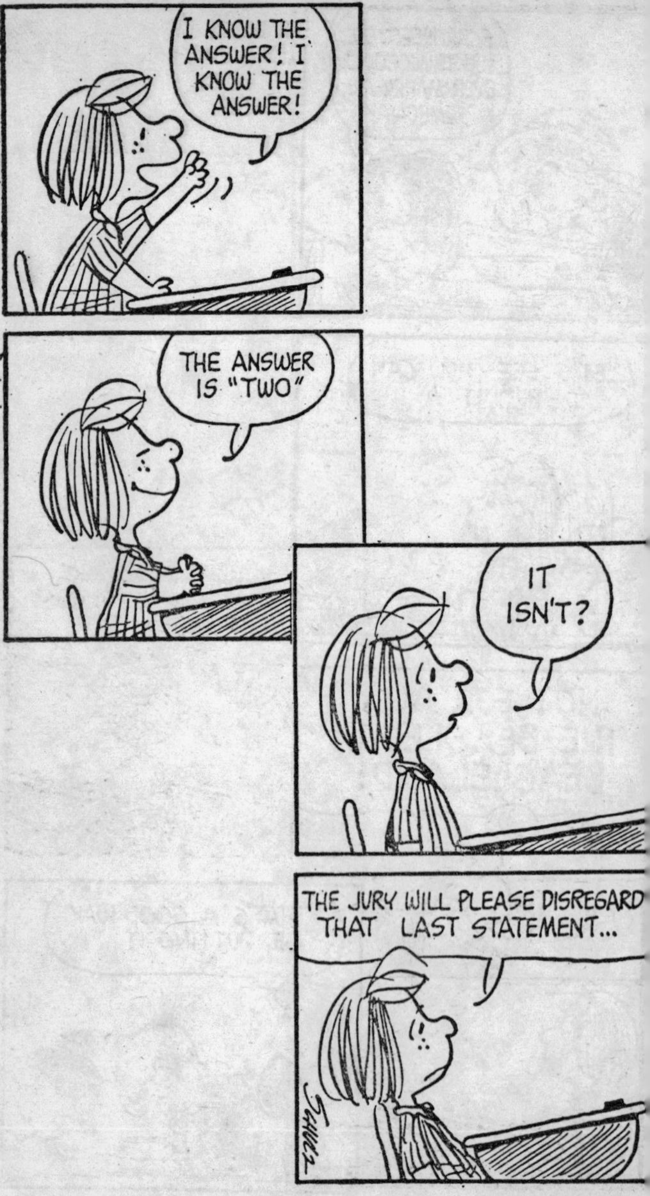
I KNOW THE ANSWER! I KNOW THE ANSWER!
THE ANSWER IS "TWO"
IT ISN'T?
THE JURY WILL PLEASE DISREGARD THAT LAST STATEMENT...
SCHULZ

I'LL NEVER GET THIS SECOND PROBLEM

JUST PUT DOWN "ELEVEN," FRANKLIN, AND DON'T WORRY ABOUT IT... THAT'S WHAT I DID..

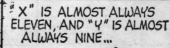

"X" IS ALMOST ALWAYS ELEVEN, AND "Y" IS ALMOST ALWAYS NINE...

ONE THING I'VE LEARNED ABOUT ALGEBRA..DON'T TAKE IT TOO SERIOUSLY...

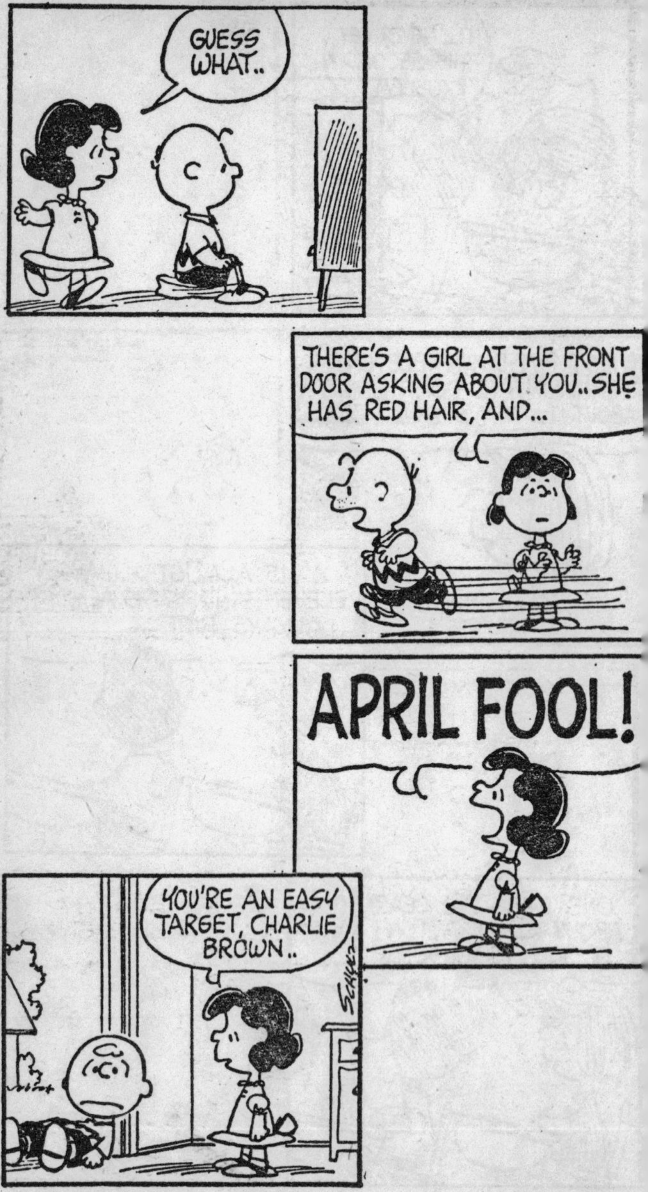
GUESS WHAT..
THERE'S A GIRL AT THE FRONT DOOR ASKING ABOUT YOU..SHE HAS RED HAIR, AND...
APRIL FOOL!
YOU'RE AN EASY TARGET, CHARLIE BROWN..
SCHULZ

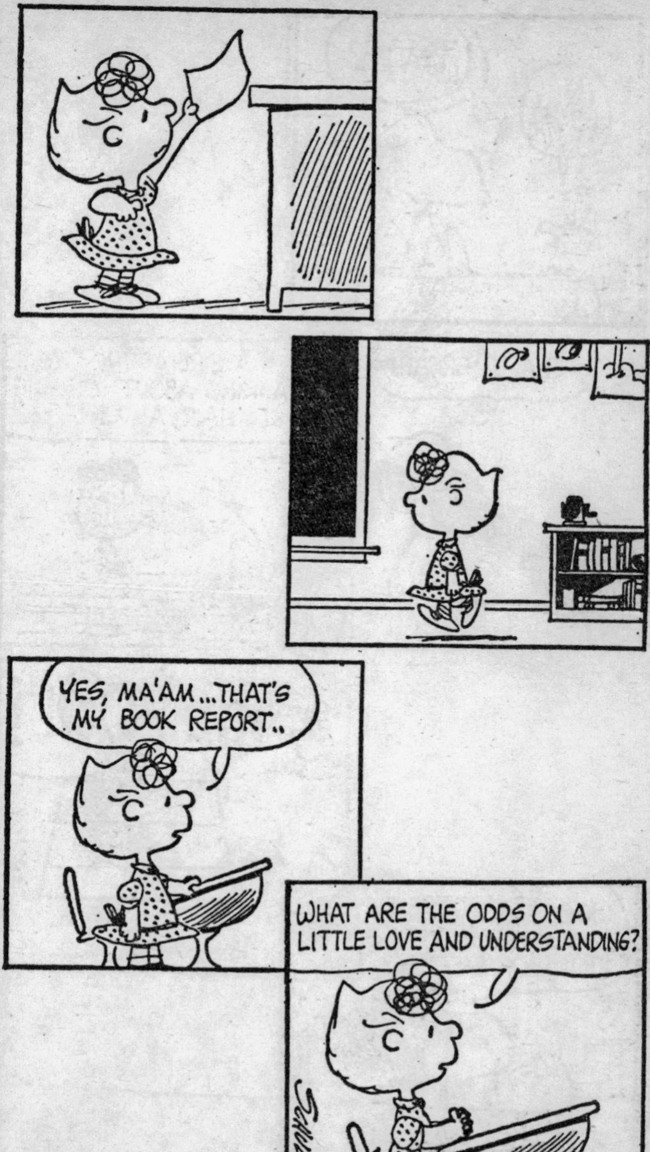
YES, MA'AM...THAT'S MY BOOK REPORT..
WHAT ARE THE ODDS ON A LITTLE LOVE AND UNDERSTANDING?
SCHULZ

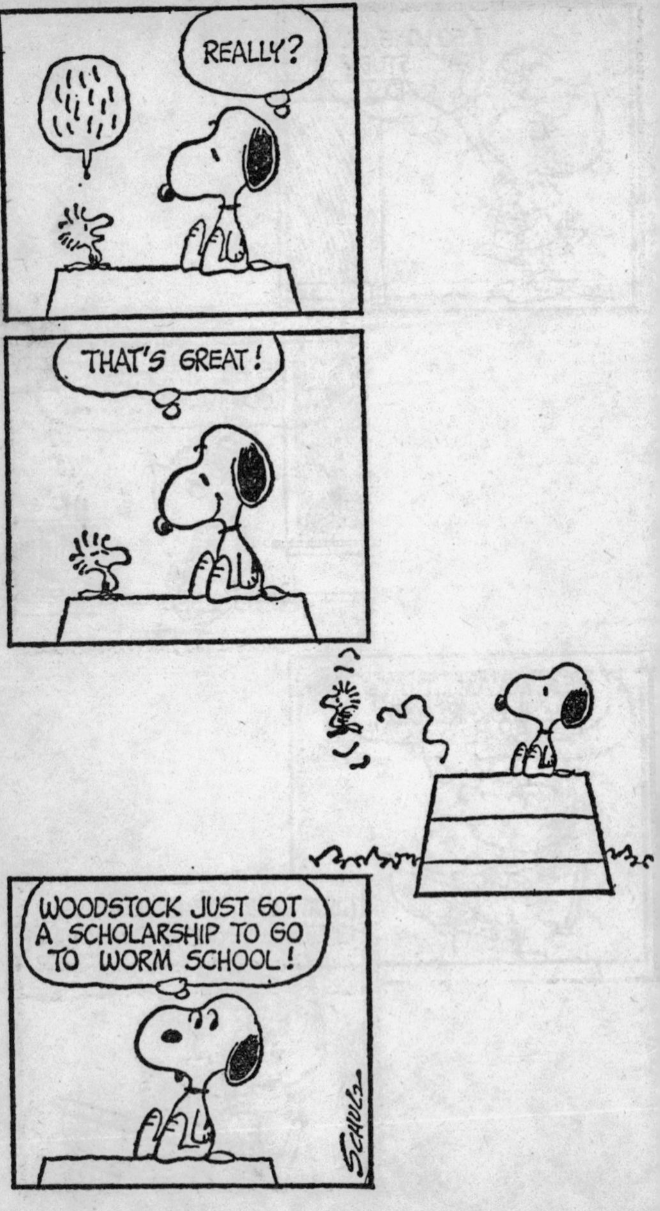
REALLY?
THAT'S GREAT!
WOODSTOCK JUST GOT A SCHOLARSHIP TO GO TO WORM SCHOOL!
SCHULZ

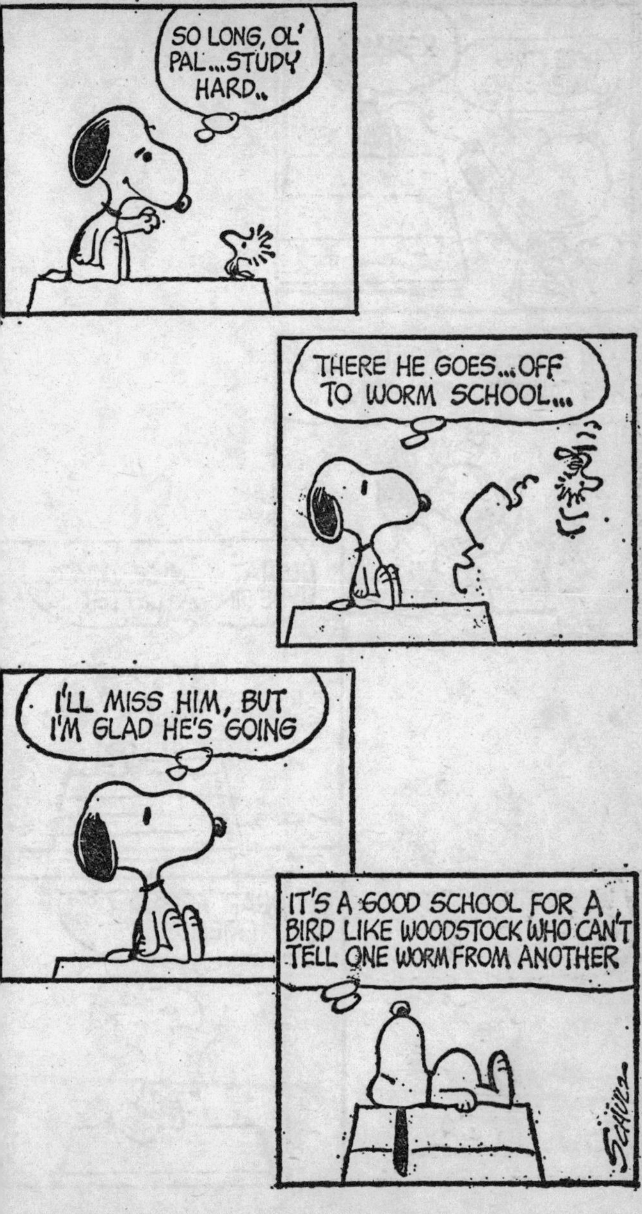
SO LONG, OL' PAL...STUDY HARD..
THERE HE GOES...OFF TO WORM SCHOOL...
I'LL MISS HIM, BUT I'M GLAD HE'S GOING
IT'S A GOOD SCHOOL FOR A BIRD LIKE WOODSTOCK WHO CAN'T TELL ONE WORM FROM ANOTHER
SCHULZ

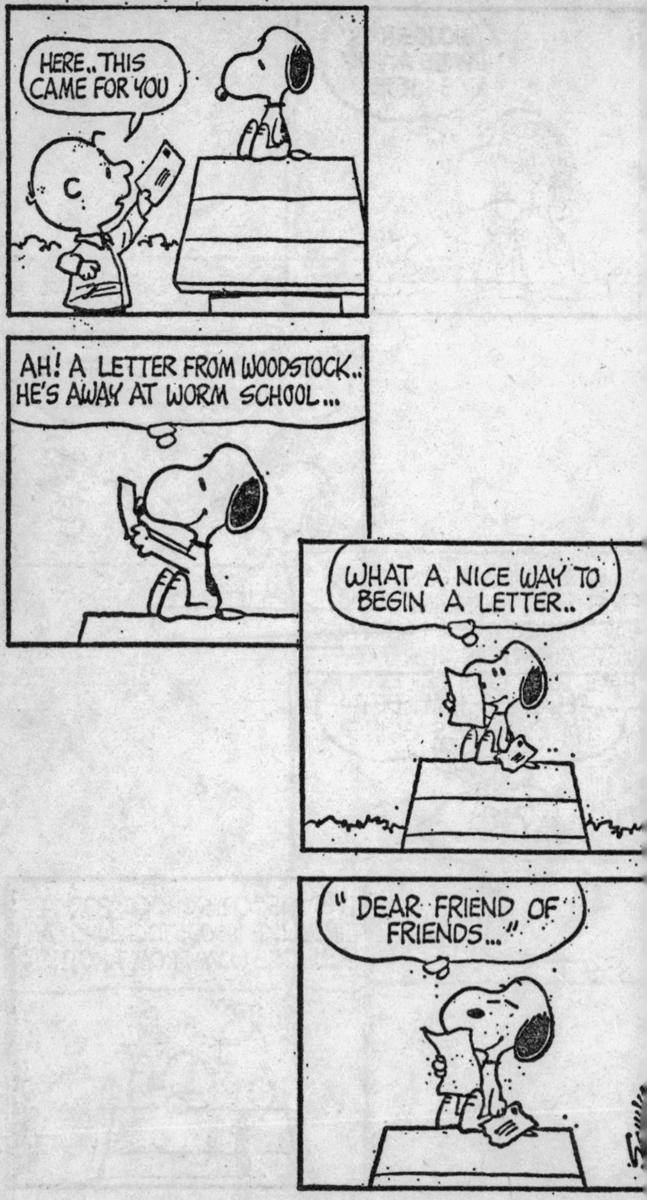
HERE.. THIS CAME FOR YOU
AH! A LETTER FROM WOODSTOCK.. HE'S AWAY AT WORM SCHOOL...
WHAT A NICE WAY TO BEGIN A LETTER..
" DEAR FRIEND OF FRIENDS..."

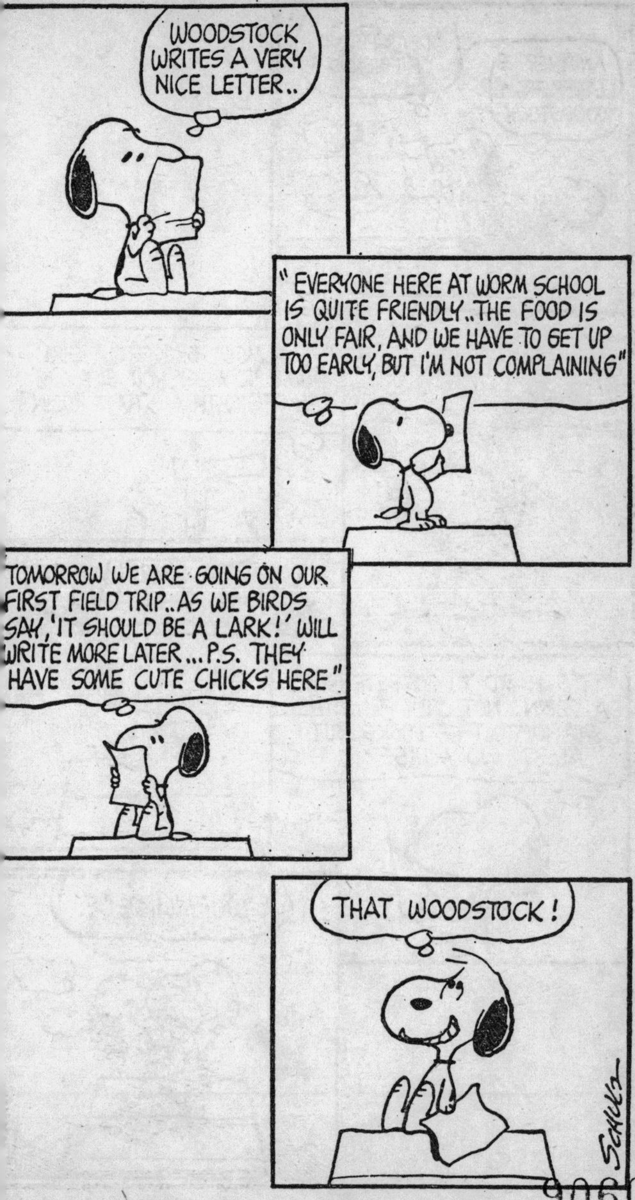
WOODSTOCK WRITES A VERY NICE LETTER..
"EVERYONE HERE AT WORM SCHOOL IS QUITE FRIENDLY..THE FOOD IS ONLY FAIR, AND WE HAVE TO GET UP TOO EARLY, BUT I'M NOT COMPLAINING"
TOMORROW WE ARE GOING ON OUR FIRST FIELD TRIP..AS WE BIRDS SAY, 'IT SHOULD BE A LARK!' WILL WRITE MORE LATER...P.S. THEY HAVE SOME CUTE CHICKS HERE"
THAT WOODSTOCK!
SCHULZ

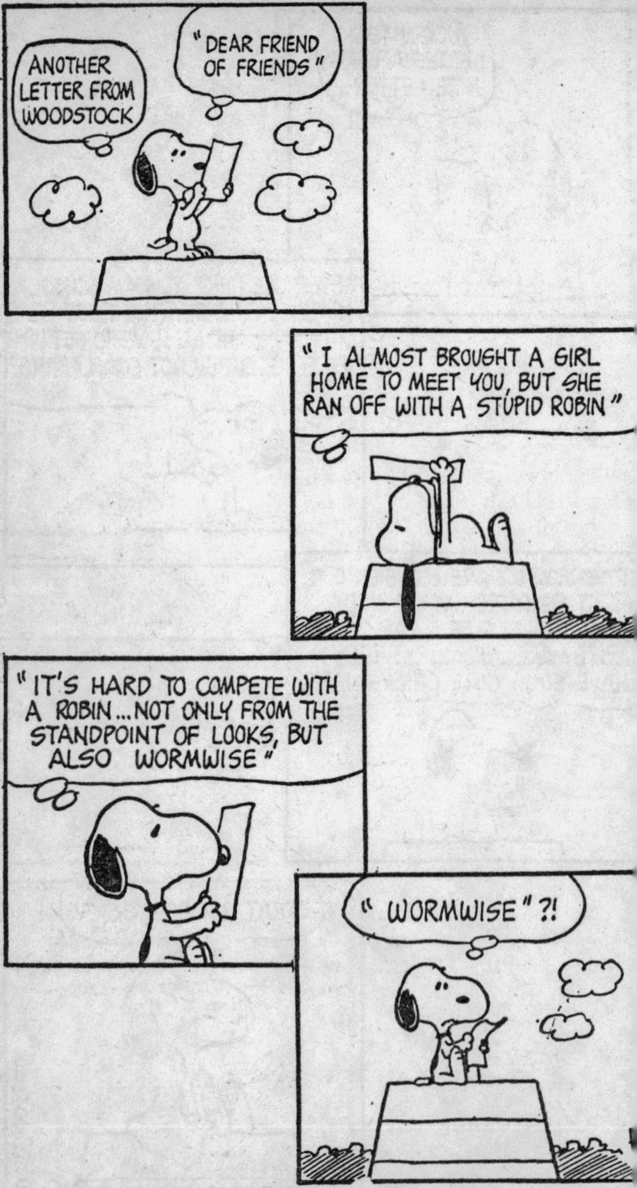
ANOTHER LETTER FROM WOODSTOCK
"DEAR FRIEND OF FRIENDS"
"I ALMOST BROUGHT A GIRL HOME TO MEET YOU, BUT SHE RAN OFF WITH A STUPID ROBIN"
"IT'S HARD TO COMPETE WITH A ROBIN...NOT ONLY FROM THE STANDPOINT OF LOOKS, BUT ALSO WORMWISE"
"WORMWISE"?!

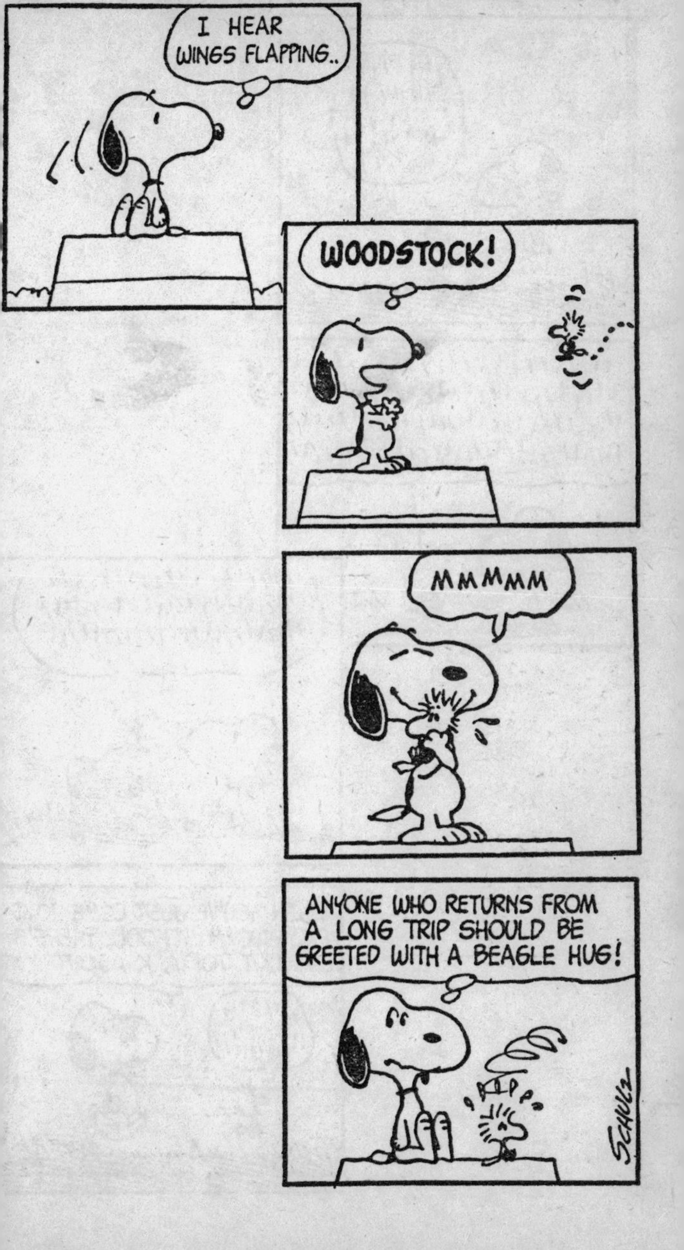
I HEAR WINGS FLAPPING..
WOODSTOCK!
MMMMM
ANYONE WHO RETURNS FROM A LONG TRIP SHOULD BE GREETED WITH A BEAGLE HUG!
SCHULZ

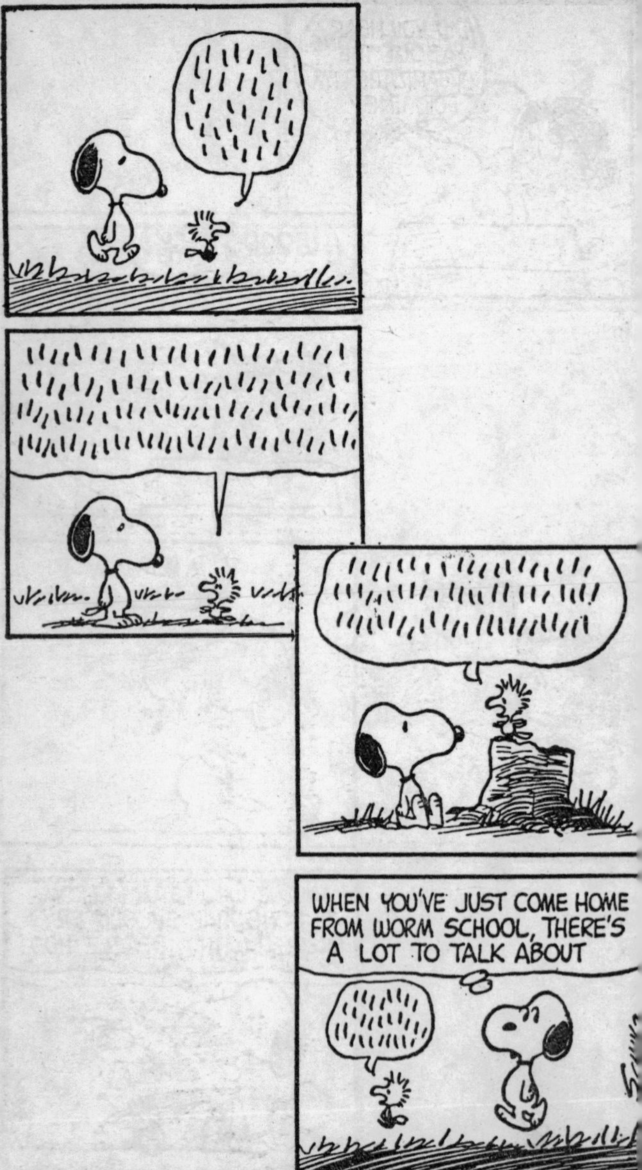
WHEN YOU'VE JUST COME HOME FROM WORM SCHOOL, THERE'S A LOT TO TALK ABOUT

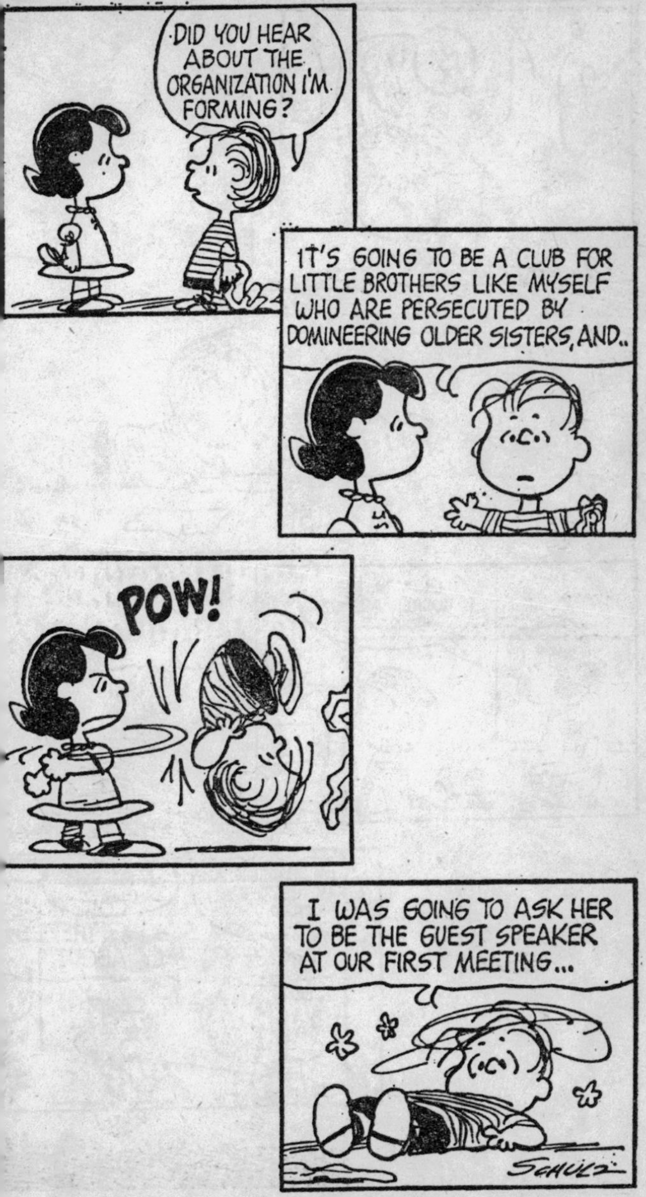
DID YOU HEAR ABOUT THE ORGANIZATION I'M FORMING?
IT'S GOING TO BE A CLUB FOR LITTLE BROTHERS LIKE MYSELF WHO ARE PERSECUTED BY DOMINEERING OLDER SISTERS, AND..
POW!
I WAS GOING TO ASK HER TO BE THE GUEST SPEAKER AT OUR FIRST MEETING...
SCHULZ

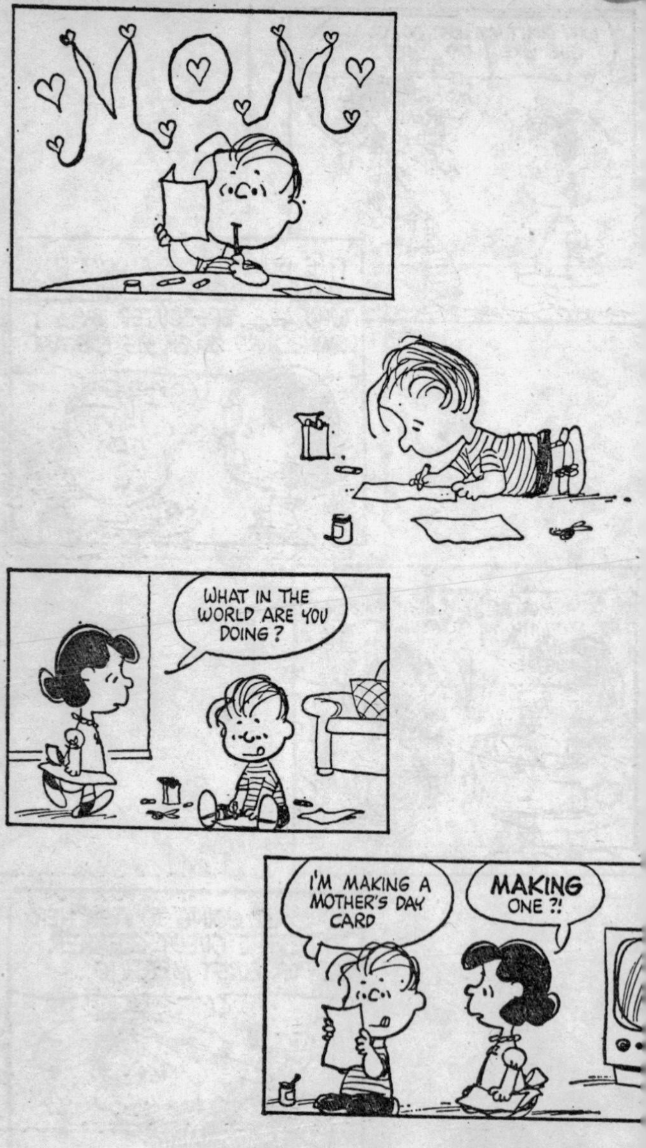
MOM
WHAT IN THE WORLD ARE YOU DOING?
I'M MAKING A MOTHER'S DAY CARD
MAKING ONE ?!

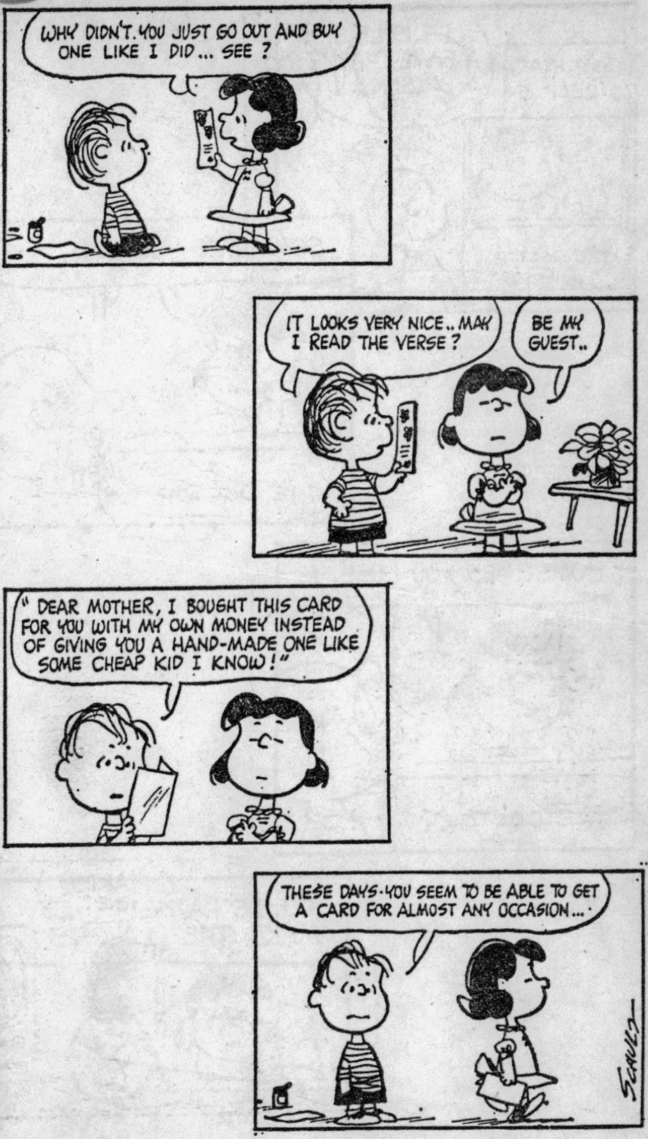
WHY DIDN'T YOU JUST GO OUT AND BUY ONE LIKE I DID... SEE ?
IT LOOKS VERY NICE.. MAY I READ THE VERSE ?
BE MY GUEST..
" DEAR MOTHER, I BOUGHT THIS CARD FOR YOU WITH MY OWN MONEY INSTEAD OF GIVING YOU A HAND-MADE ONE LIKE SOME CHEAP KID I KNOW ! "
THESE DAYS YOU SEEM TO BE ABLE TO GET A CARD FOR ALMOST ANY OCCASION...
SCHULZ

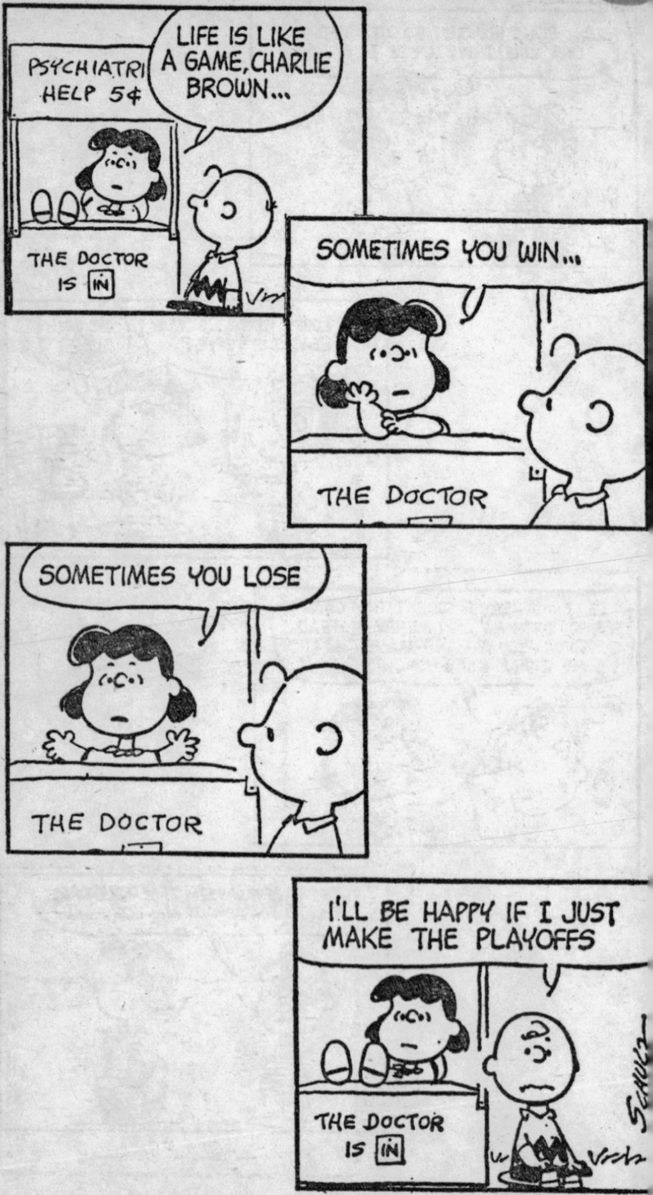
PSYCHIATRI HELP 5¢
LIFE IS LIKE A GAME, CHARLIE BROWN...
THE DOCTOR IS IN
SOMETIMES YOU WIN...
THE DOCTOR
SOMETIMES YOU LOSE
THE DOCTOR
I'LL BE HAPPY IF I JUST MAKE THE PLAYOFFS
THE DOCTOR IS IN
SCHULZ

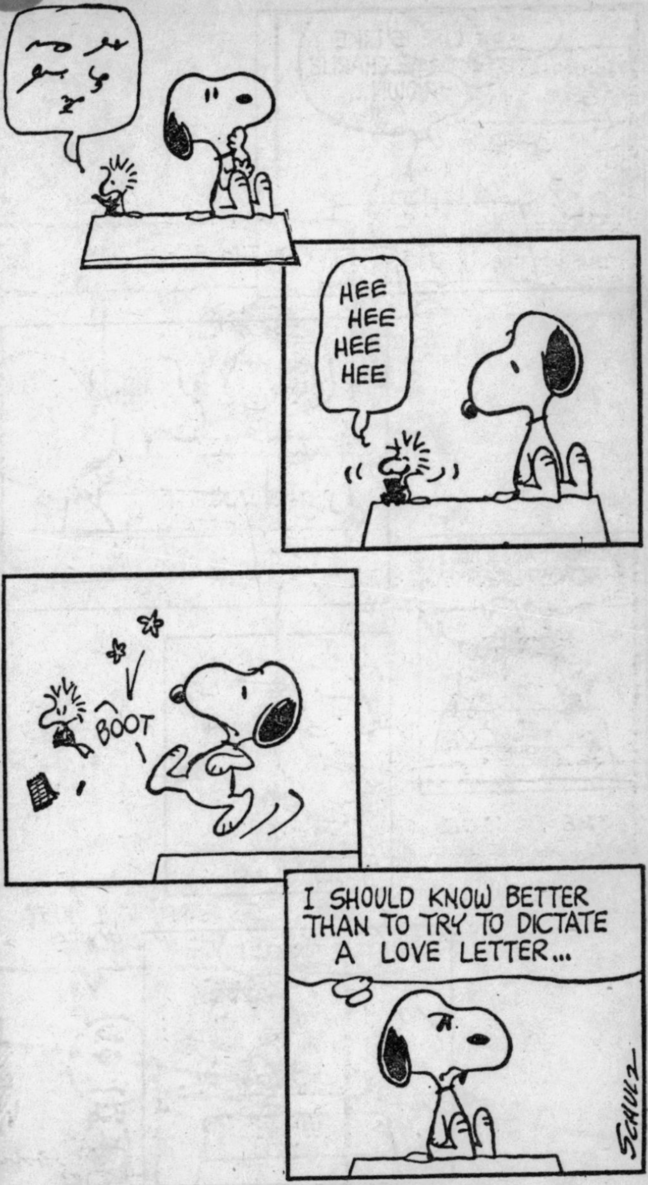
HEE
HEE
HEE
HEE
BOOT
I SHOULD KNOW BETTER THAN TO TRY TO DICTATE A LOVE LETTER...
SCHULZ

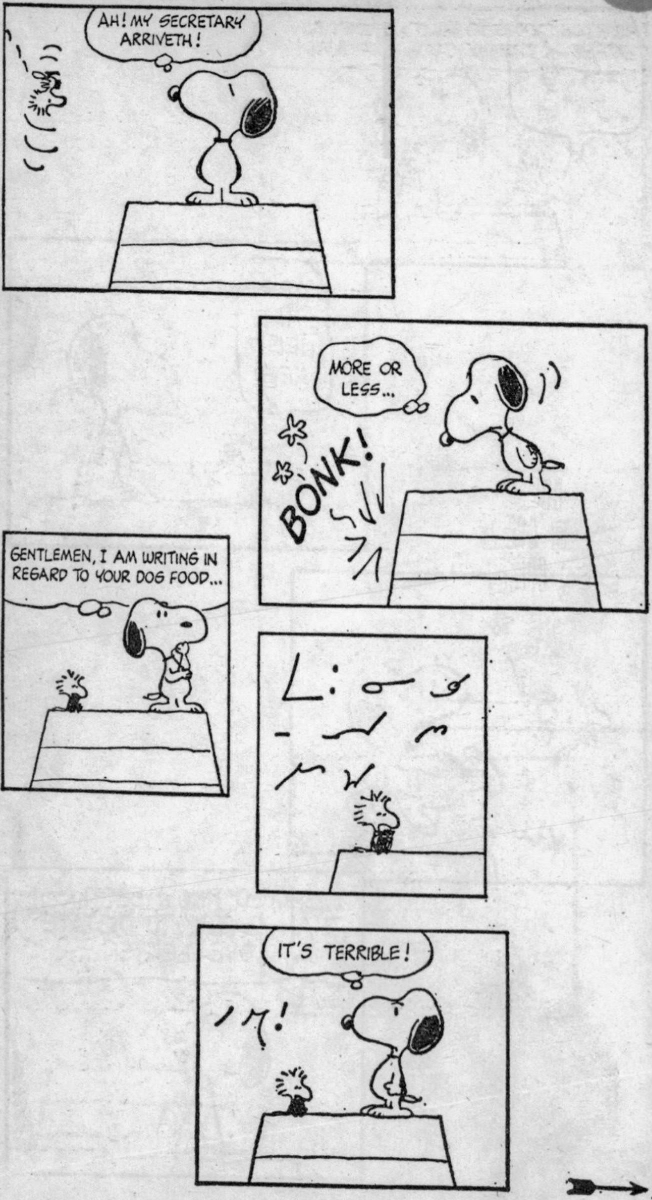
AH! MY SECRETARY ARRIVETH!
MORE OR LESS...
BONK!
GENTLEMEN, I AM WRITING IN REGARD TO YOUR DOG FOOD...
IT'S TERRIBLE!

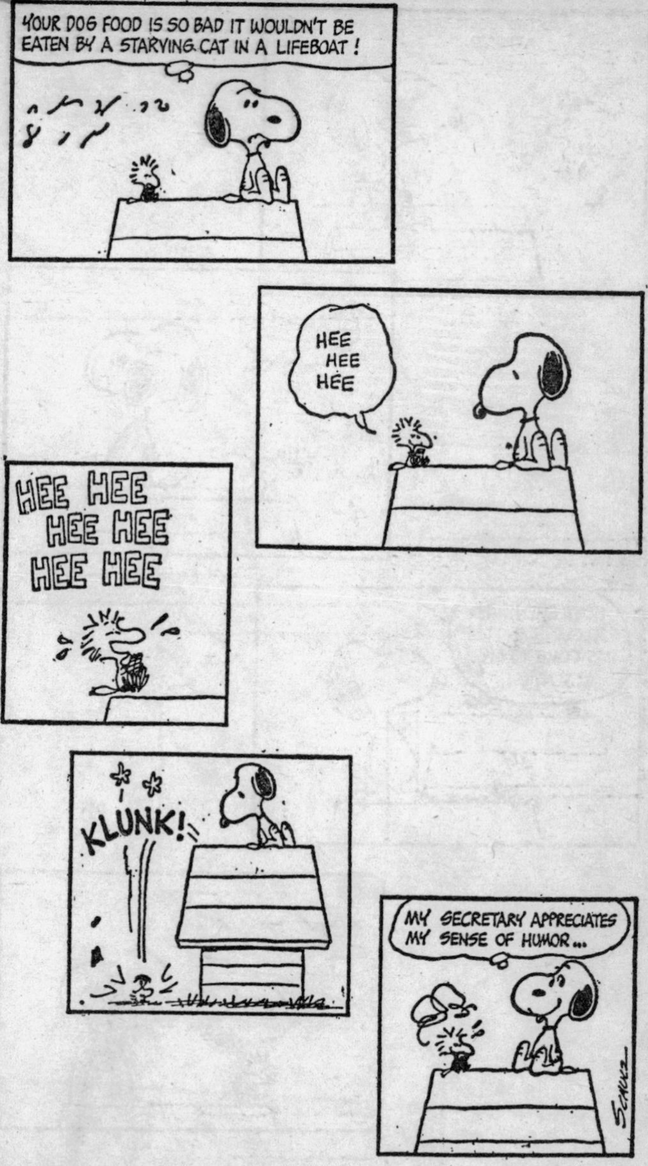
YOUR DOG FOOD IS SO BAD IT WOULDN'T BE EATEN BY A STARVING CAT IN A LIFEBOAT!
HEE HEE HEE
HEE HEE HEE HEE HEE HEE
KLUNK!
MY SECRETARY APPRECIATES MY SENSE OF HUMOR...
SCHULZ

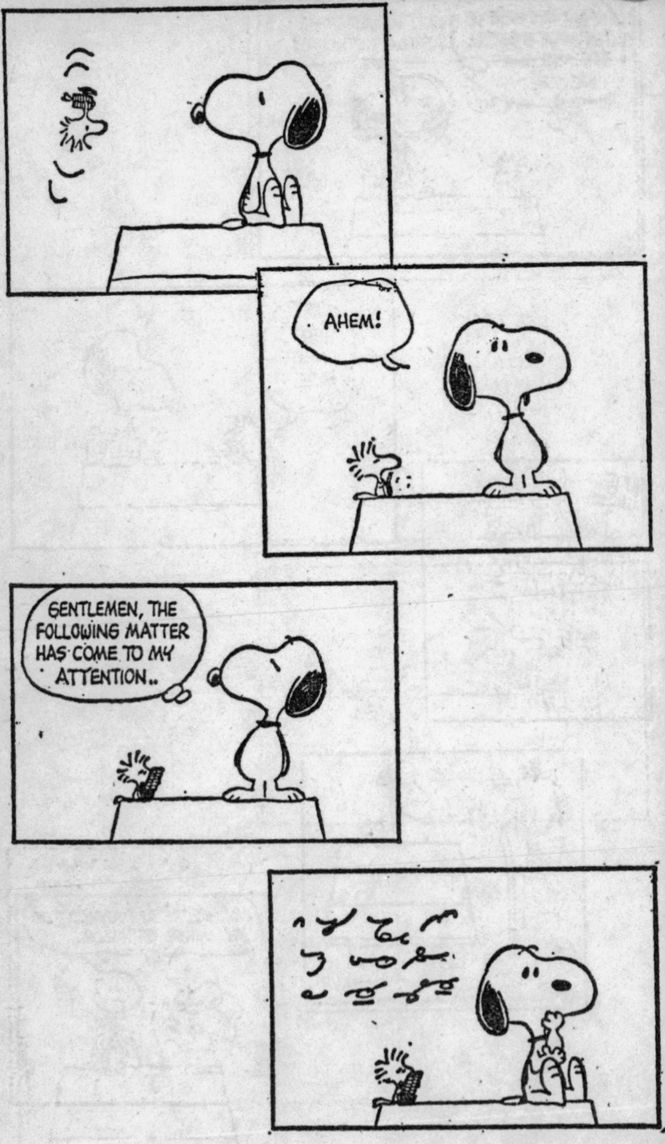
AHEM!
GENTLEMEN, THE FOLLOWING MATTER HAS COME TO MY ATTENTION..

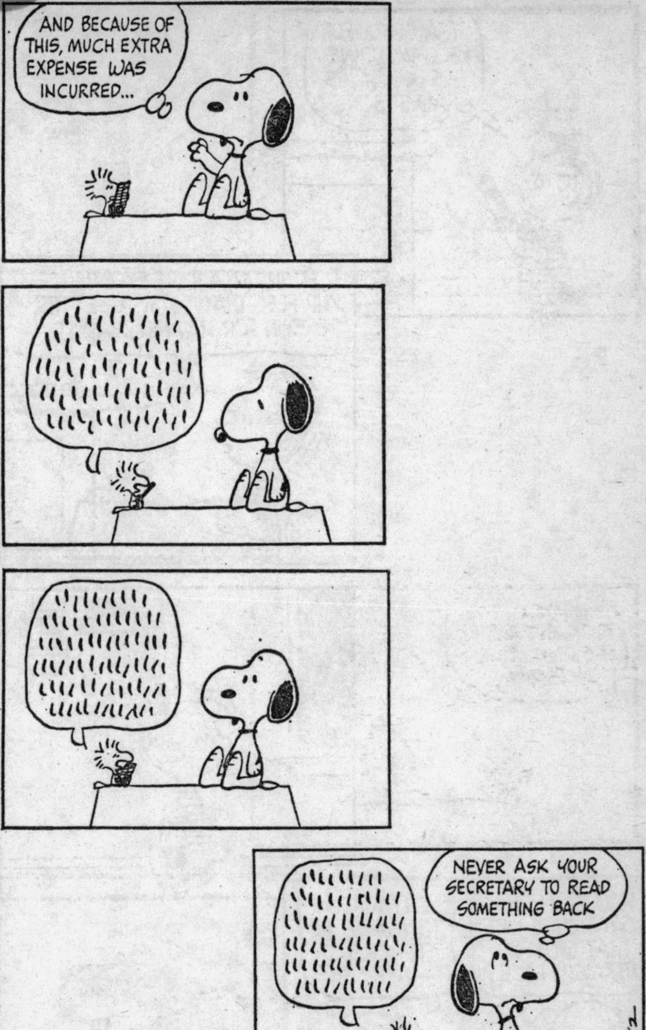
AND BECAUSE OF THIS, MUCH EXTRA EXPENSE WAS INCURRED...
NEVER ASK YOUR SECRETARY TO READ SOMETHING BACK
SCHULZ

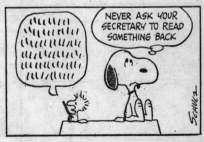

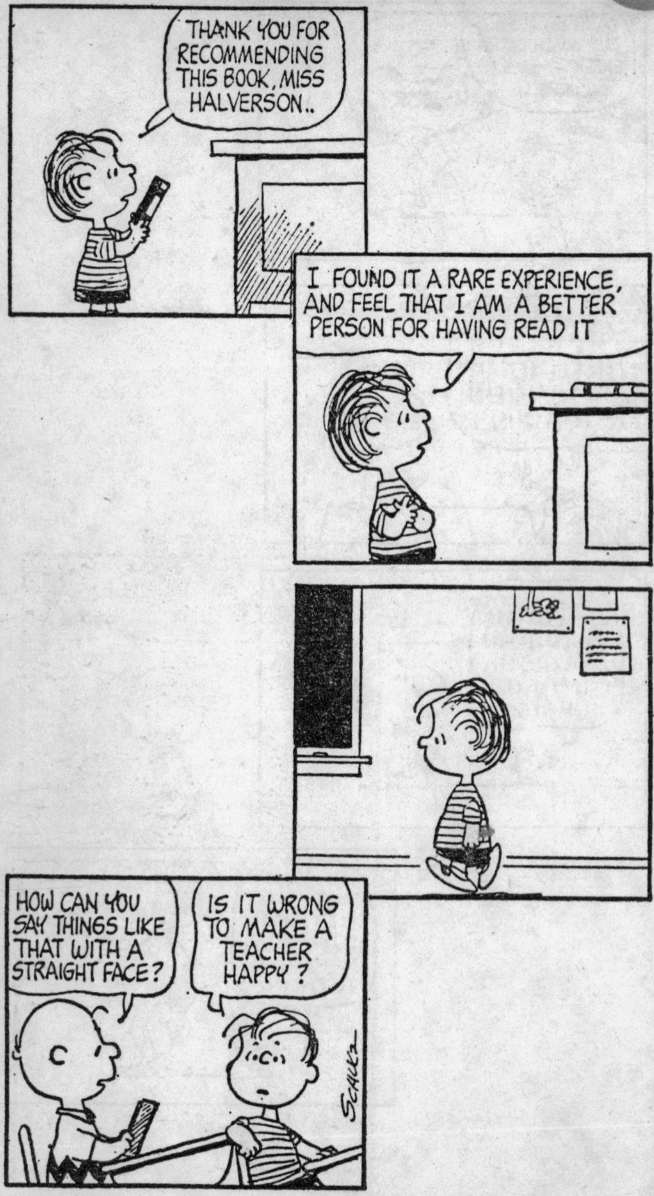
THANK YOU FOR RECOMMENDING THIS BOOK, MISS HALVERSON..
I FOUND IT A RARE EXPERIENCE, AND FEEL THAT I AM A BETTER PERSON FOR HAVING READ IT
HOW CAN YOU SAY THINGS LIKE THAT WITH A STRAIGHT FACE?
IS IT WRONG TO MAKE A TEACHER HAPPY?
SCHULZ

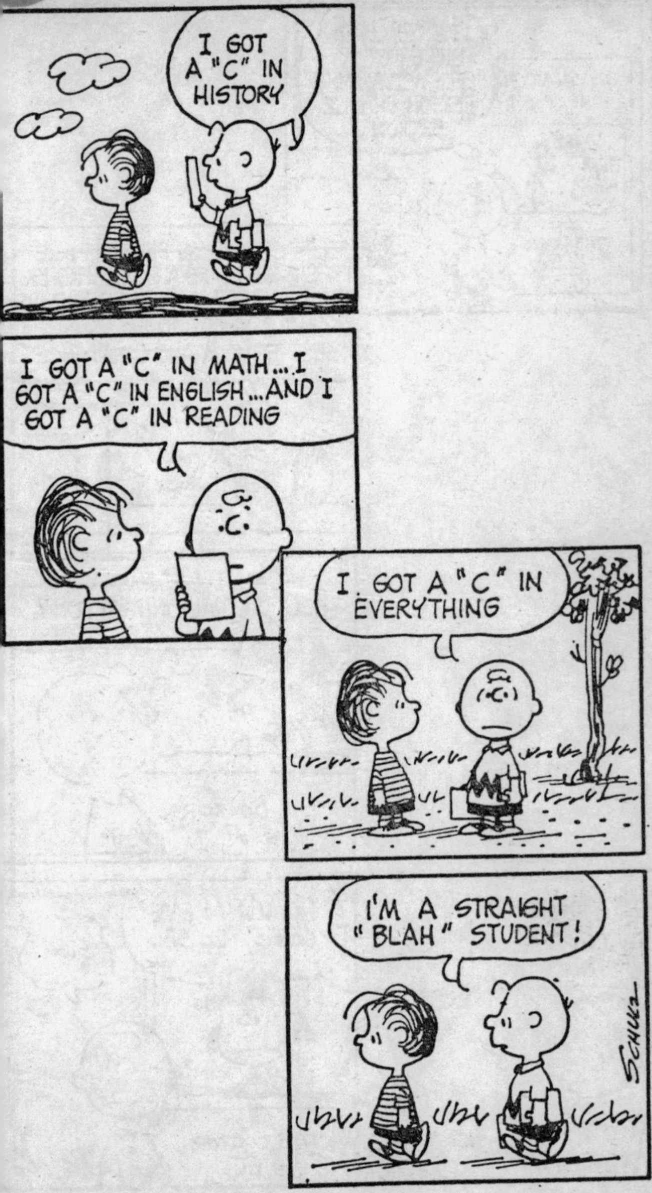
I GOT A "C" IN HISTORY
I GOT A "C" IN MATH...I GOT A "C" IN ENGLISH...AND I GOT A "C" IN READING
I GOT A "C" IN EVERYTHING
I'M A STRAIGHT "BLAH" STUDENT!
SCHULZ

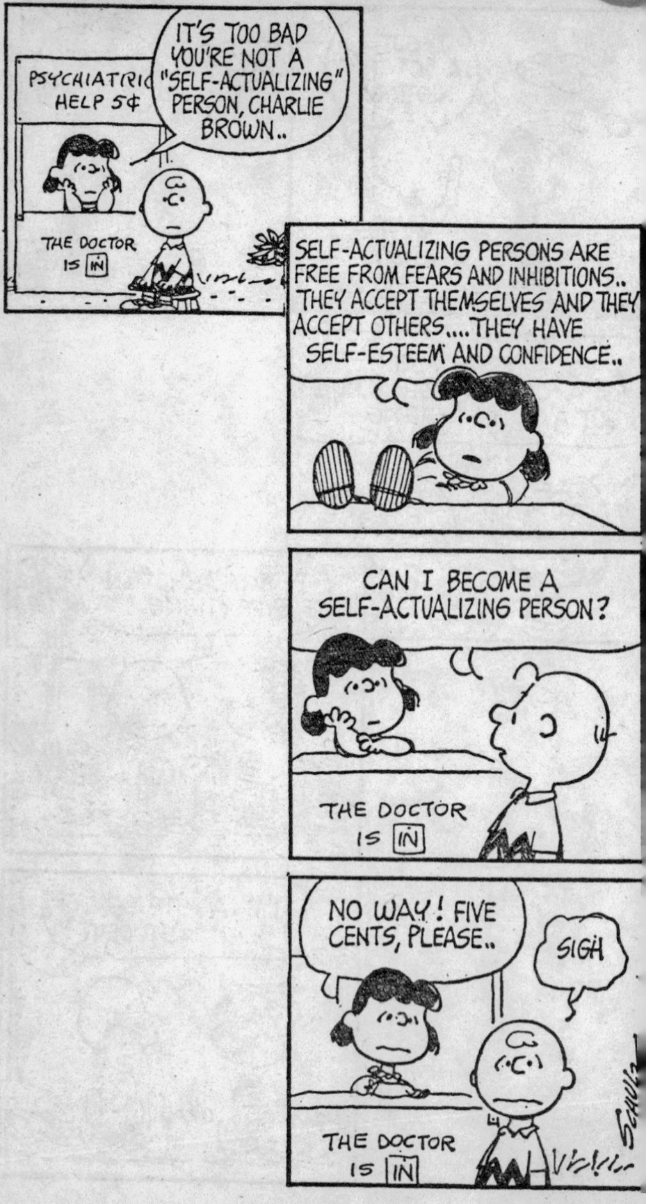
PSYCHIATRIC HELP 5¢
IT'S TOO BAD YOU'RE NOT A "SELF-ACTUALIZING" PERSON, CHARLIE BROWN..
THE DOCTOR IS IN
SELF-ACTUALIZING PERSONS ARE FREE FROM FEARS AND INHIBITIONS.. THEY ACCEPT THEMSELVES AND THEY ACCEPT OTHERS....THEY HAVE SELF-ESTEEM AND CONFIDENCE..
CAN I BECOME A SELF-ACTUALIZING PERSON?
THE DOCTOR IS IN
NO WAY! FIVE CENTS, PLEASE..
SIGH
THE DOCTOR IS IN
SCHULZ

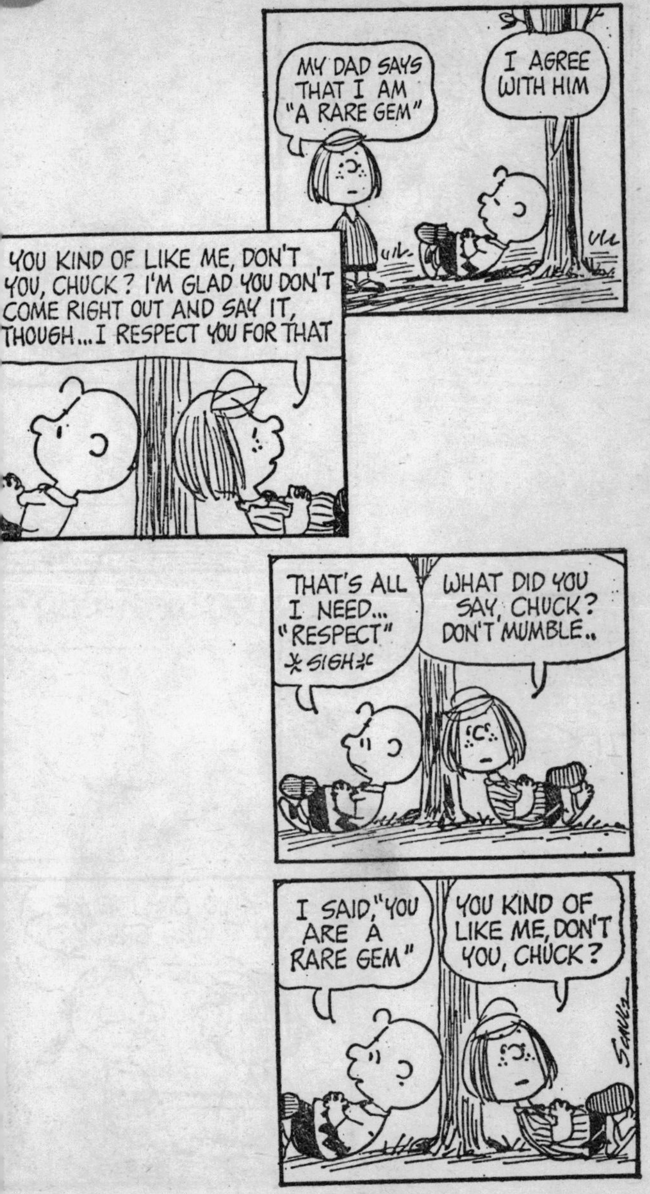
MY DAD SAYS THAT I AM "A RARE GEM"
I AGREE WITH HIM
YOU KIND OF LIKE ME, DON'T YOU, CHUCK? I'M GLAD YOU DON'T COME RIGHT OUT AND SAY IT, THOUGH...I RESPECT YOU FOR THAT
THAT'S ALL I NEED... "RESPECT" *SIGH*
WHAT DID YOU SAY, CHUCK? DON'T MUMBLE..
I SAID, "YOU ARE A RARE GEM"
YOU KIND OF LIKE ME, DON'T YOU, CHUCK?

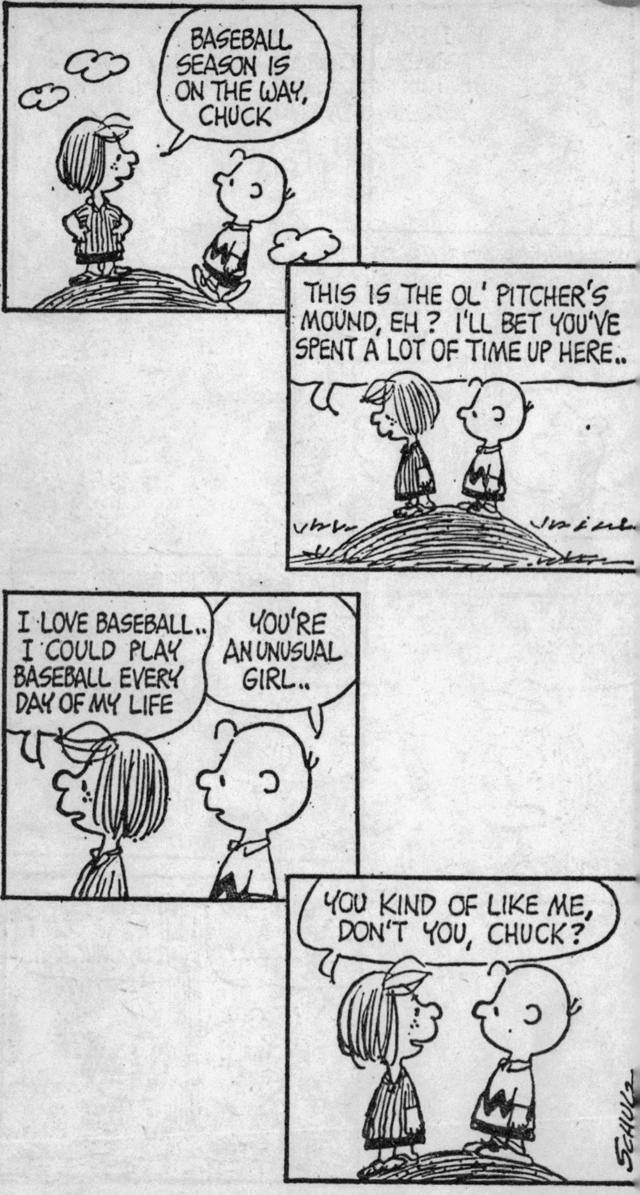
BASEBALL SEASON IS ON THE WAY, CHUCK
THIS IS THE OL' PITCHER'S MOUND, EH ? I'LL BET YOU'VE SPENT A LOT OF TIME UP HERE..
I LOVE BASEBALL.. I COULD PLAY BASEBALL EVERY DAY OF MY LIFE
YOU'RE AN UNUSUAL GIRL..
YOU KIND OF LIKE ME, DON'T YOU, CHUCK?
SCHULZ

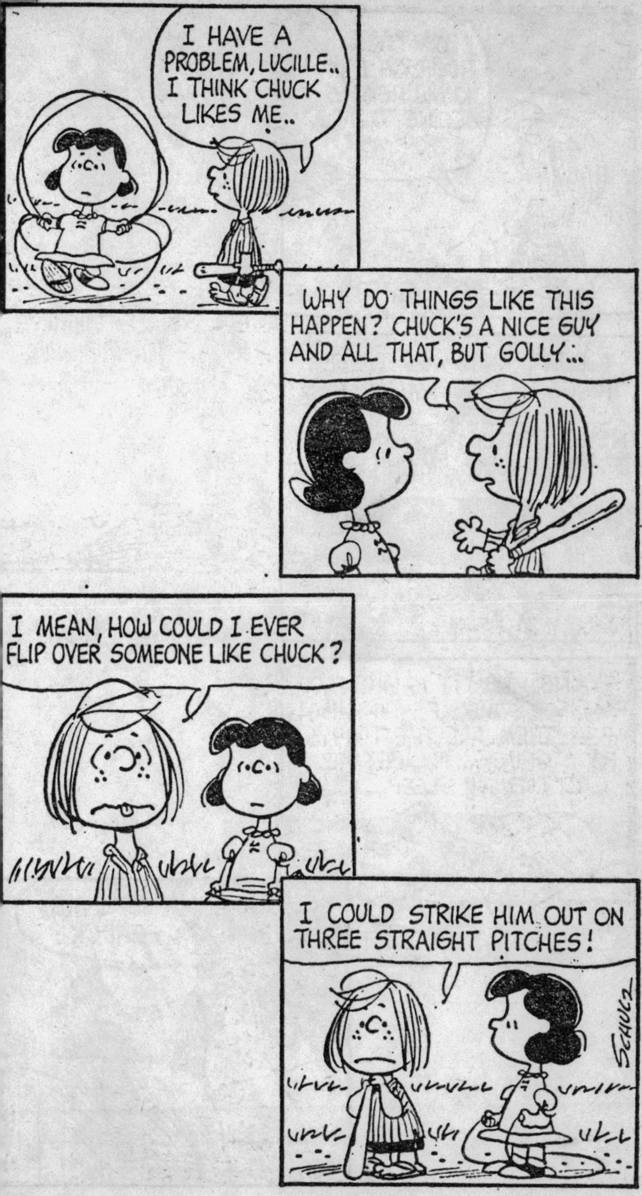
I HAVE A PROBLEM, LUCILLE.. I THINK CHUCK LIKES ME..
WHY DO THINGS LIKE THIS HAPPEN? CHUCK'S A NICE GUY AND ALL THAT, BUT GOLLY...
I MEAN, HOW COULD I EVER FLIP OVER SOMEONE LIKE CHUCK?
I COULD STRIKE HIM OUT ON THREE STRAIGHT PITCHES!
SCHULZ

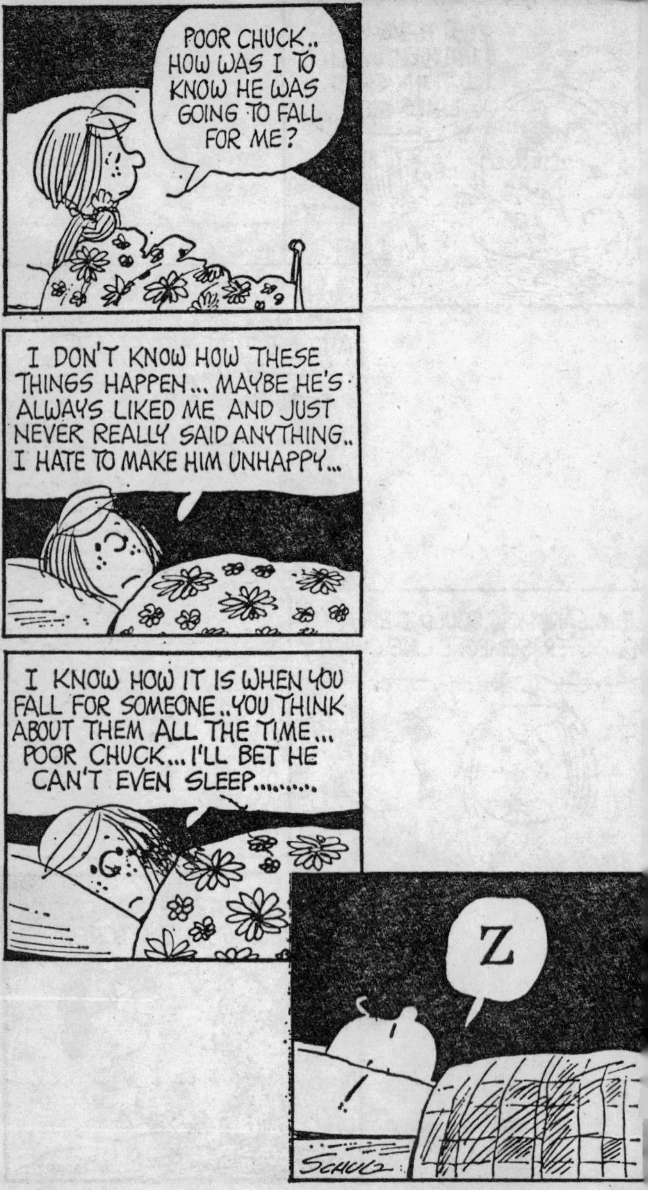
POOR CHUCK.. HOW WAS I TO KNOW HE WAS GOING TO FALL FOR ME?
I DON'T KNOW HOW THESE THINGS HAPPEN... MAYBE HE'S ALWAYS LIKED ME AND JUST NEVER REALLY SAID ANYTHING.. I HATE TO MAKE HIM UNHAPPY...
I KNOW HOW IT IS WHEN YOU FALL FOR SOMEONE..YOU THINK ABOUT THEM ALL THE TIME... POOR CHUCK... I'LL BET HE CAN'T EVEN SLEEP.........
Z
SCHULZ

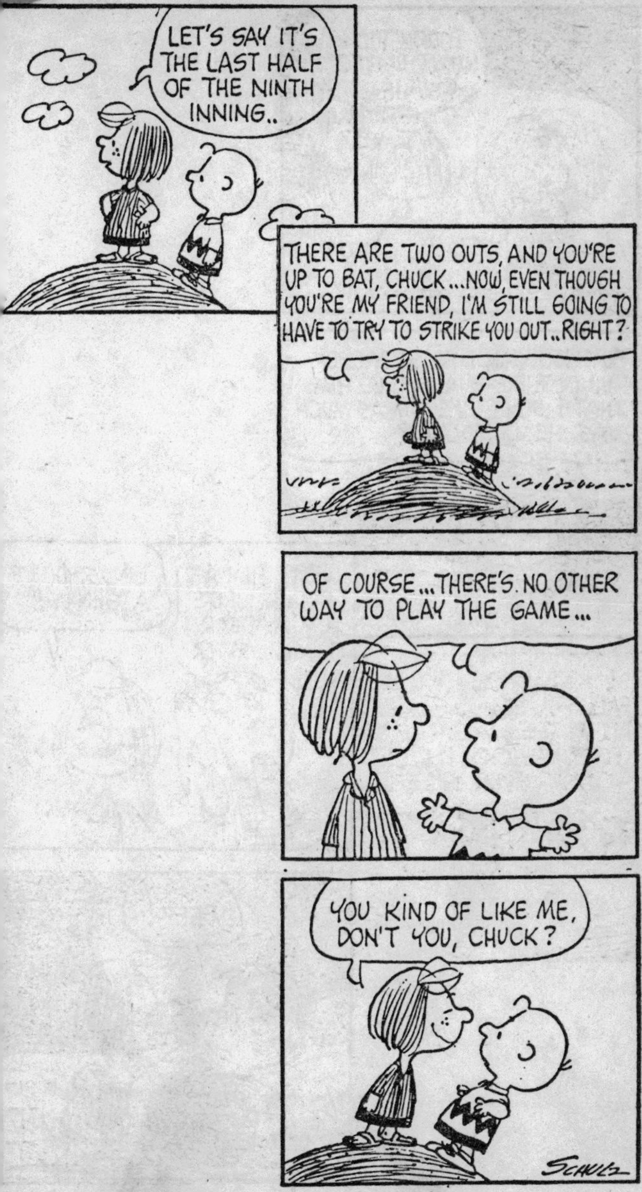
LET'S SAY IT'S THE LAST HALF OF THE NINTH INNING..
THERE ARE TWO OUTS, AND YOU'RE UP TO BAT, CHUCK...NOW, EVEN THOUGH YOU'RE MY FRIEND, I'M STILL GOING TO HAVE TO TRY TO STRIKE YOU OUT..RIGHT?
OF COURSE...THERE'S NO OTHER WAY TO PLAY THE GAME...
YOU KIND OF LIKE ME, DON'T YOU, CHUCK?
SCHULZ

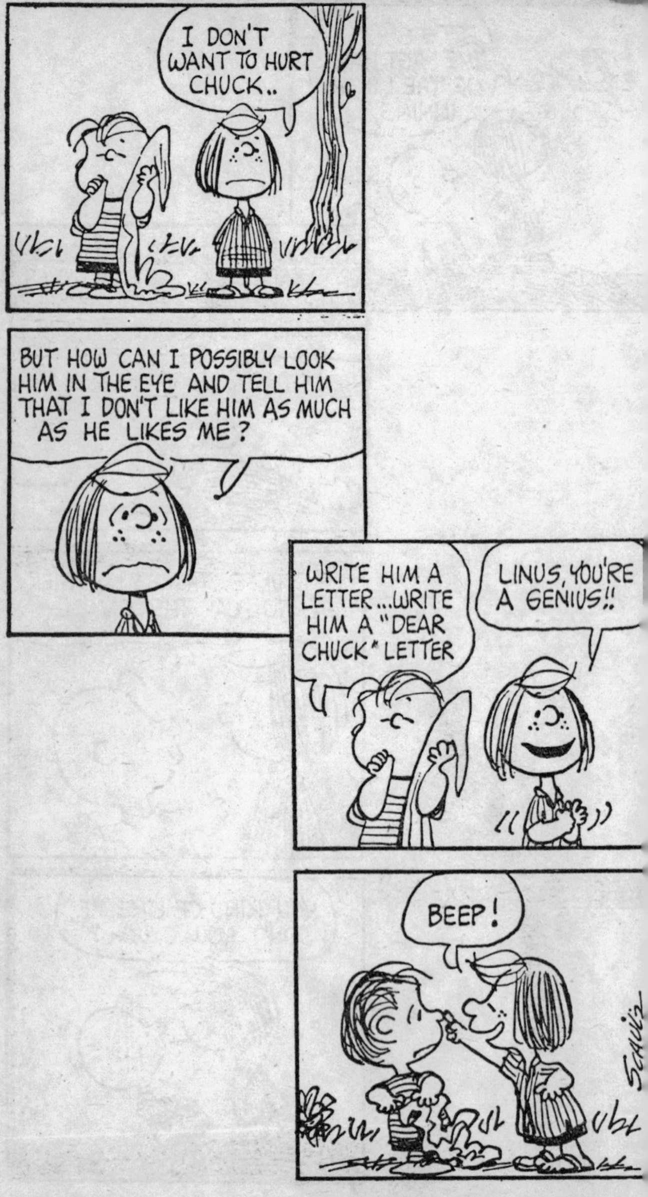
I DON'T WANT TO HURT CHUCK..
BUT HOW CAN I POSSIBLY LOOK HIM IN THE EYE AND TELL HIM THAT I DON'T LIKE HIM AS MUCH AS HE LIKES ME?
WRITE HIM A LETTER...WRITE HIM A "DEAR CHUCK" LETTER
LINUS, YOU'RE A GENIUS!!
BEEP!
SCHULZ

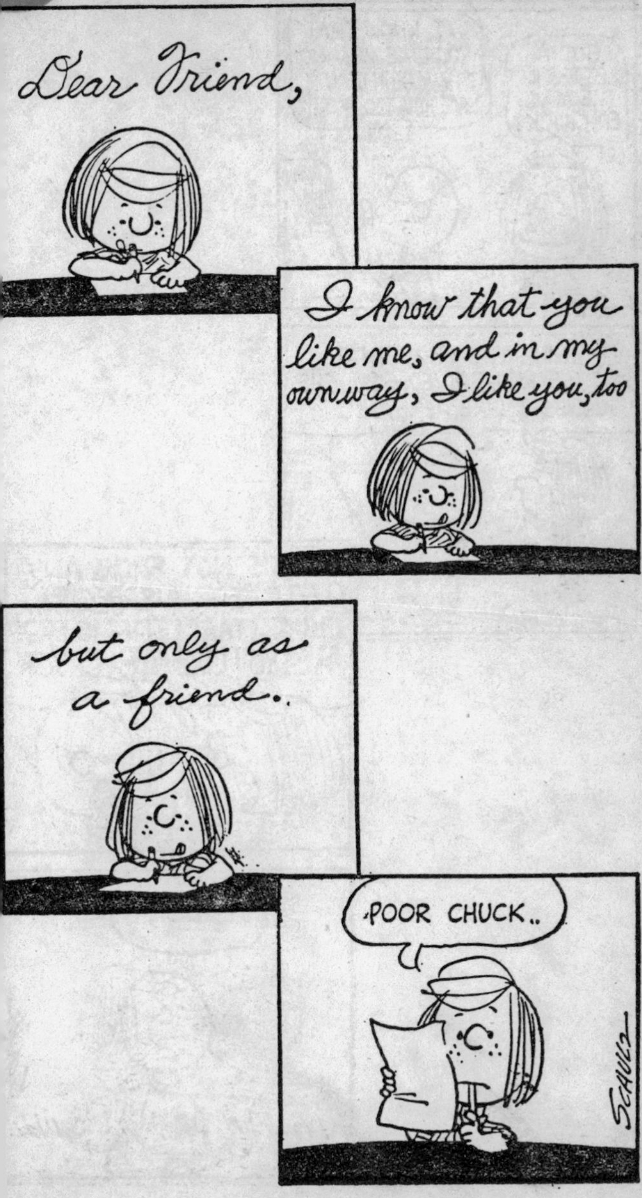
Dear Friend,
I know that you like me, and in my own way, I like you, too
but only as a friend..
POOR CHUCK..
SCHULZ

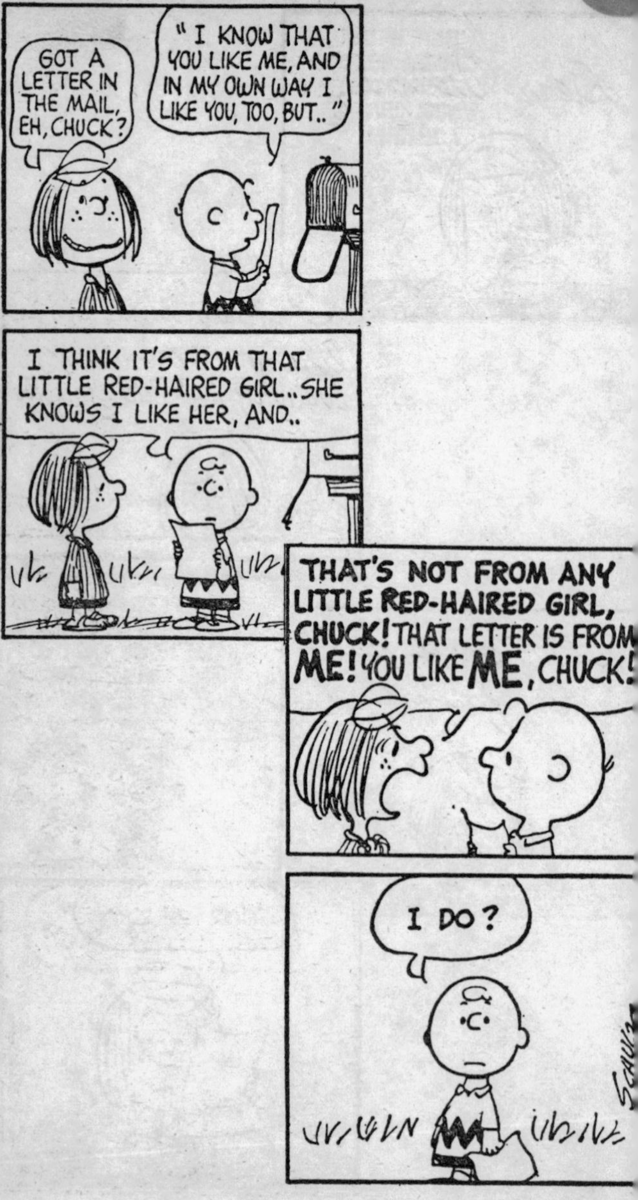
GOT A LETTER IN THE MAIL, EH, CHUCK?
"I KNOW THAT YOU LIKE ME, AND IN MY OWN WAY I LIKE YOU, TOO, BUT.."
I THINK IT'S FROM THAT LITTLE RED-HAIRED GIRL..SHE KNOWS I LIKE HER, AND..
THAT'S NOT FROM ANY LITTLE RED-HAIRED GIRL, CHUCK! THAT LETTER IS FROM ME! YOU LIKE ME, CHUCK!
I DO?

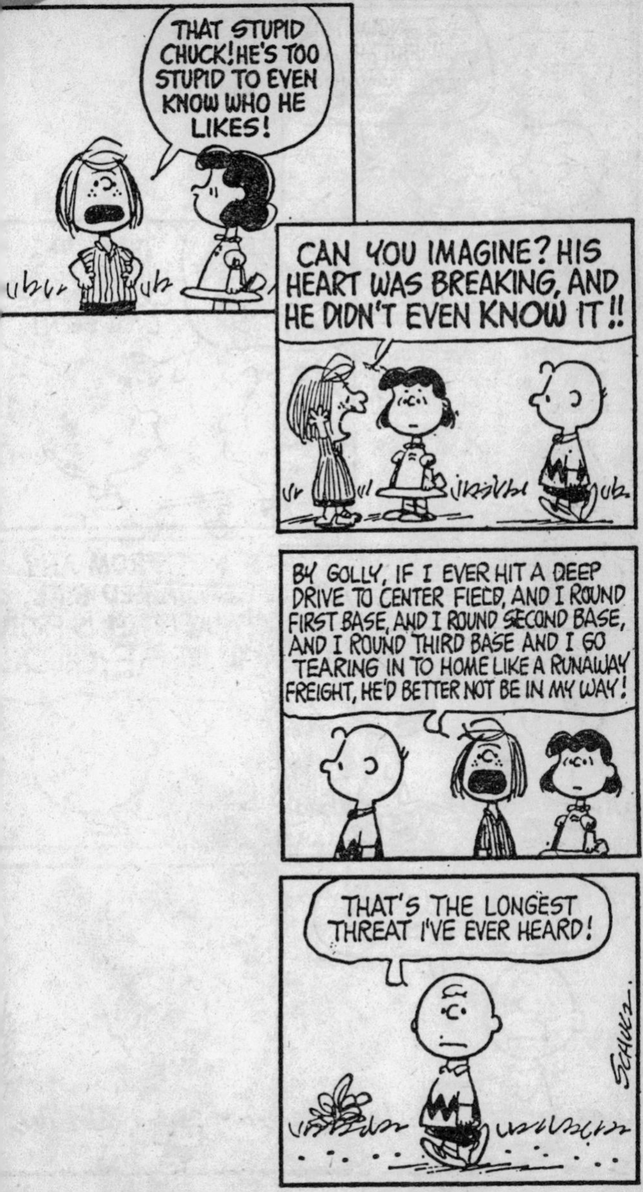
THAT STUPID CHUCK! HE'S TOO STUPID TO EVEN KNOW WHO HE LIKES!
CAN YOU IMAGINE? HIS HEART WAS BREAKING, AND HE DIDN'T EVEN KNOW IT!!
BY GOLLY, IF I EVER HIT A DEEP DRIVE TO CENTER FIELD, AND I ROUND FIRST BASE, AND I ROUND SECOND BASE, AND I ROUND THIRD BASE AND I GO TEARING IN TO HOME LIKE A RUNAWAY FREIGHT, HE'D BETTER NOT BE IN MY WAY!
THAT'S THE LONGEST THREAT I'VE EVER HEARD!
SCHULZ

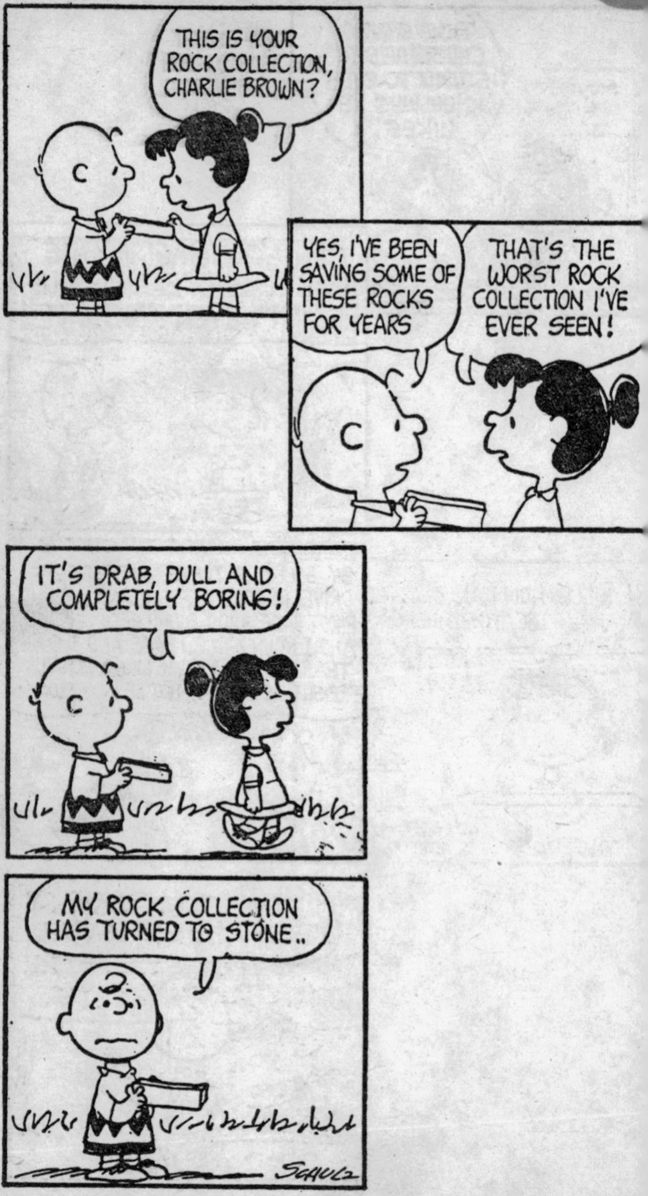
THIS IS YOUR ROCK COLLECTION, CHARLIE BROWN?
YES, I'VE BEEN SAVING SOME OF THESE ROCKS FOR YEARS
THAT'S THE WORST ROCK COLLECTION I'VE EVER SEEN!
IT'S DRAB, DULL AND COMPLETELY BORING!
MY ROCK COLLECTION HAS TURNED TO STONE..
SCHULZ

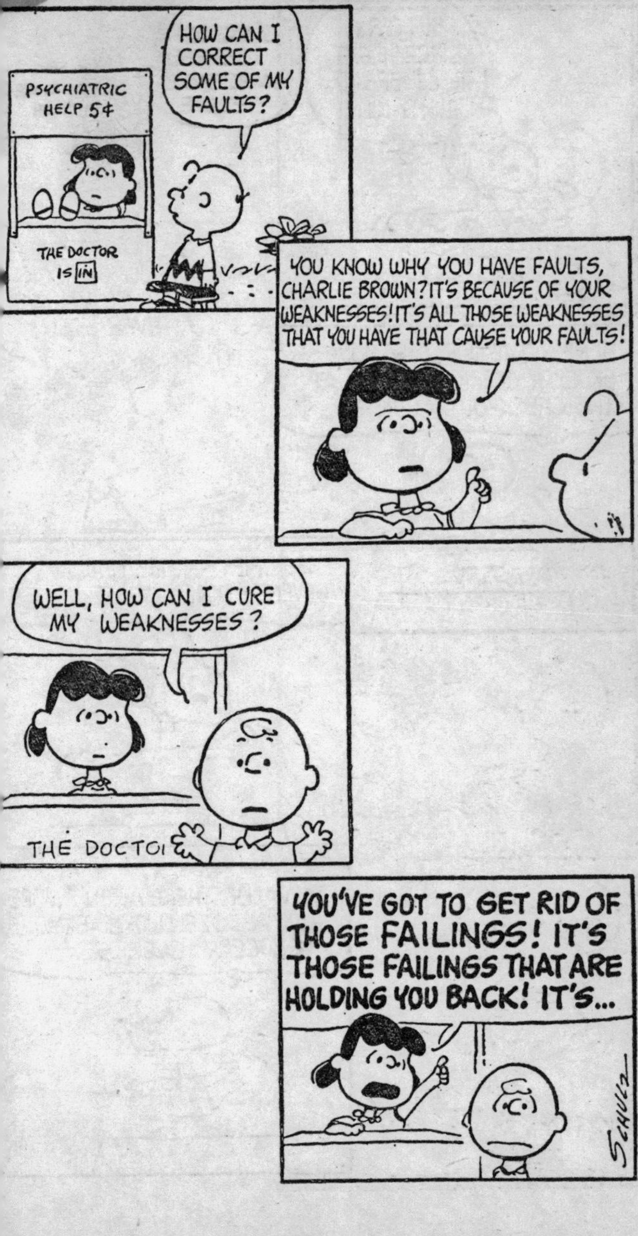
PSYCHIATRIC HELP 5¢
HOW CAN I CORRECT SOME OF MY FAULTS?
THE DOCTOR IS IN
YOU KNOW WHY YOU HAVE FAULTS, CHARLIE BROWN? IT'S BECAUSE OF YOUR WEAKNESSES! IT'S ALL THOSE WEAKNESSES THAT YOU HAVE THAT CAUSE YOUR FAULTS!
WELL, HOW CAN I CURE MY WEAKNESSES?
THE DOCTO
YOU'VE GOT TO GET RID OF THOSE FAILINGS! IT'S THOSE FAILINGS THAT ARE HOLDING YOU BACK! IT'S...
SCHULZ

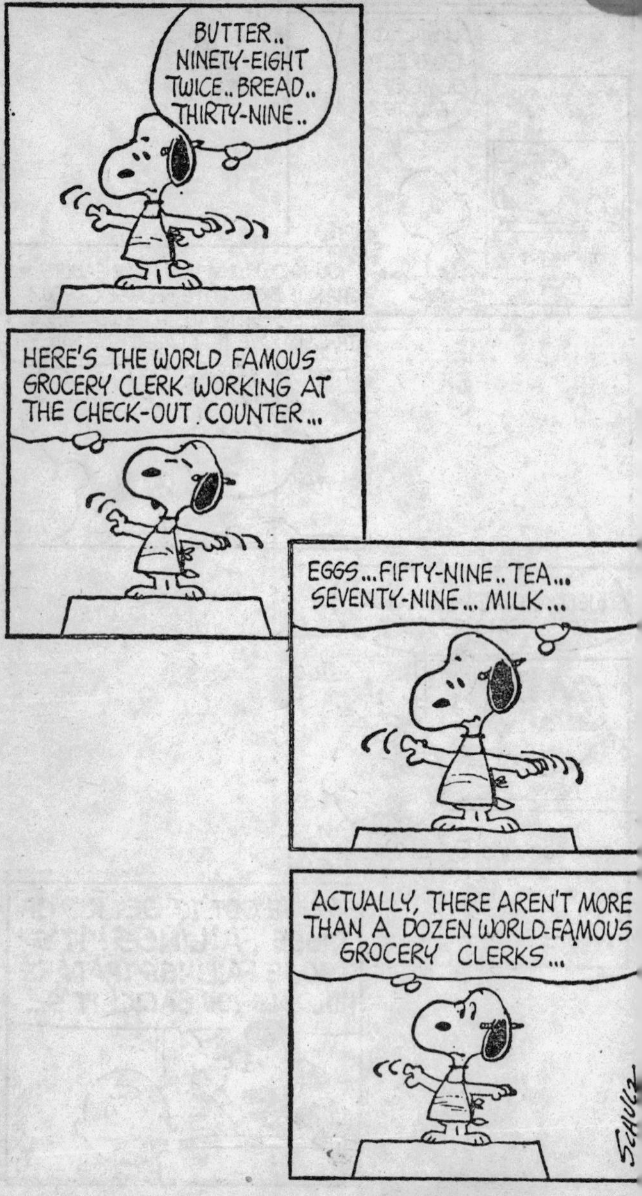
BUTTER.. NINETY-EIGHT TWICE.. BREAD.. THIRTY-NINE..
HERE'S THE WORLD FAMOUS GROCERY CLERK WORKING AT THE CHECK-OUT COUNTER...
EGGS...FIFTY-NINE..TEA... SEVENTY-NINE... MILK...
ACTUALLY, THERE AREN'T MORE THAN A DOZEN WORLD-FAMOUS GROCERY CLERKS...
SCHULZ

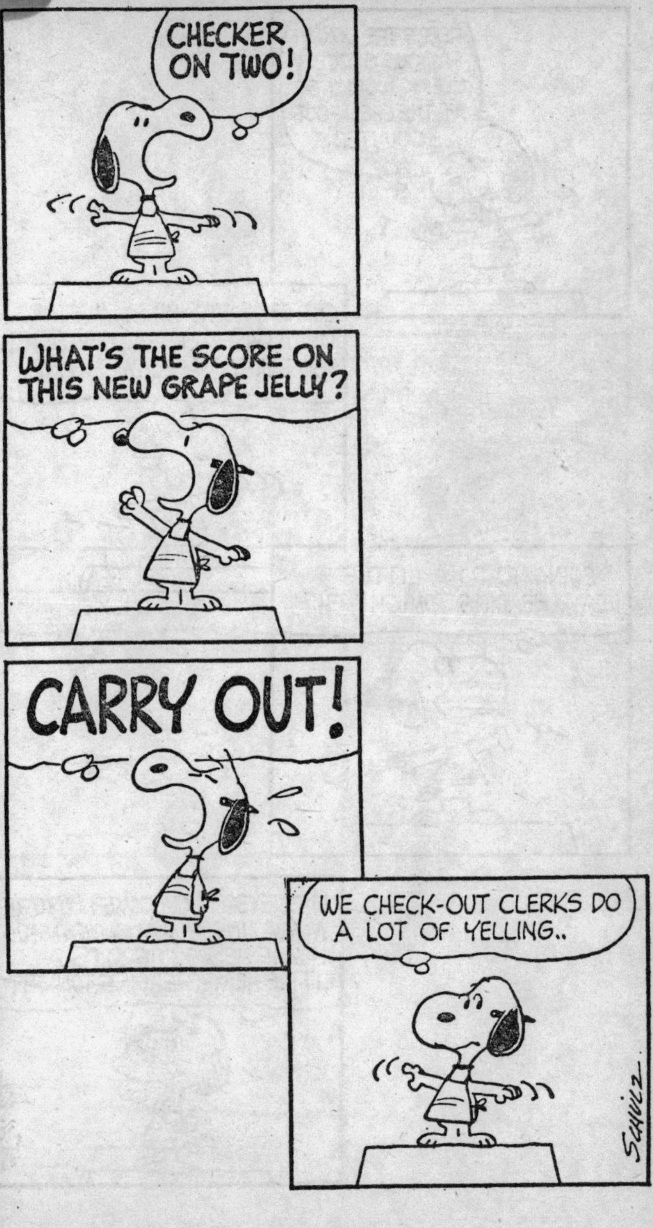
CHECKER ON TWO!
WHAT'S THE SCORE ON THIS NEW GRAPE JELLY?
CARRY OUT!
WE CHECK-OUT CLERKS DO A LOT OF YELLING..
SCHULZ

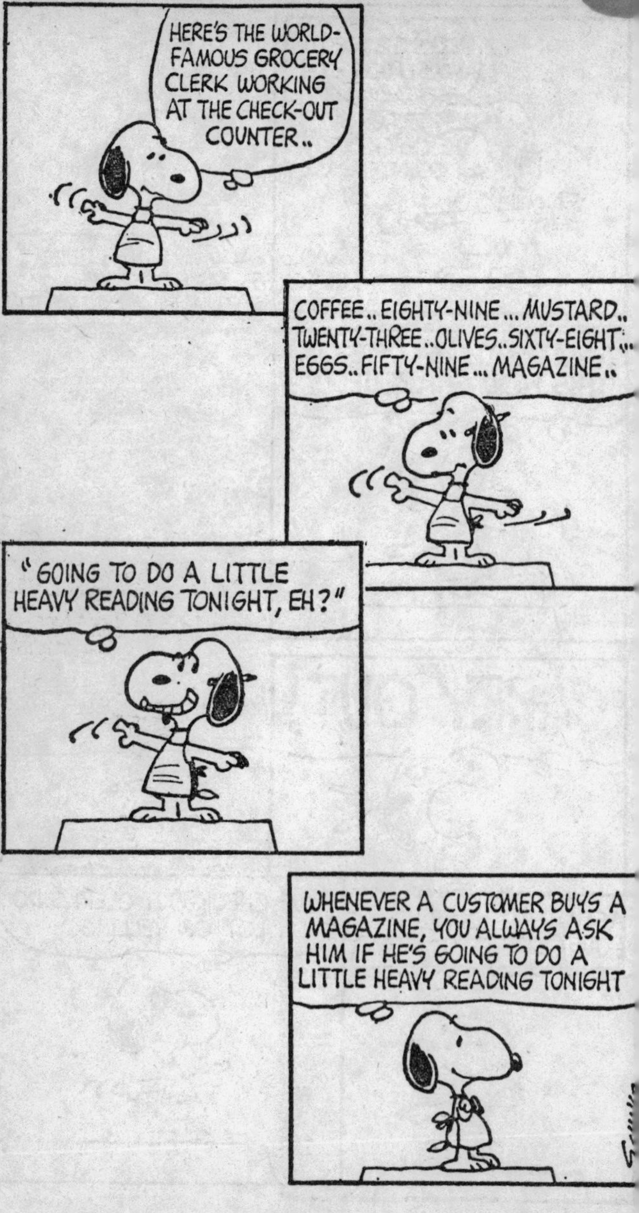
HERE'S THE WORLD-FAMOUS GROCERY CLERK WORKING AT THE CHECK-OUT COUNTER..
COFFEE.. EIGHTY-NINE... MUSTARD.. TWENTY-THREE..OLIVES..SIXTY-EIGHT... EGGS.. FIFTY-NINE... MAGAZINE..
"GOING TO DO A LITTLE HEAVY READING TONIGHT, EH?"
WHENEVER A CUSTOMER BUYS A MAGAZINE, YOU ALWAYS ASK HIM IF HE'S GOING TO DO A LITTLE HEAVY READING TONIGHT

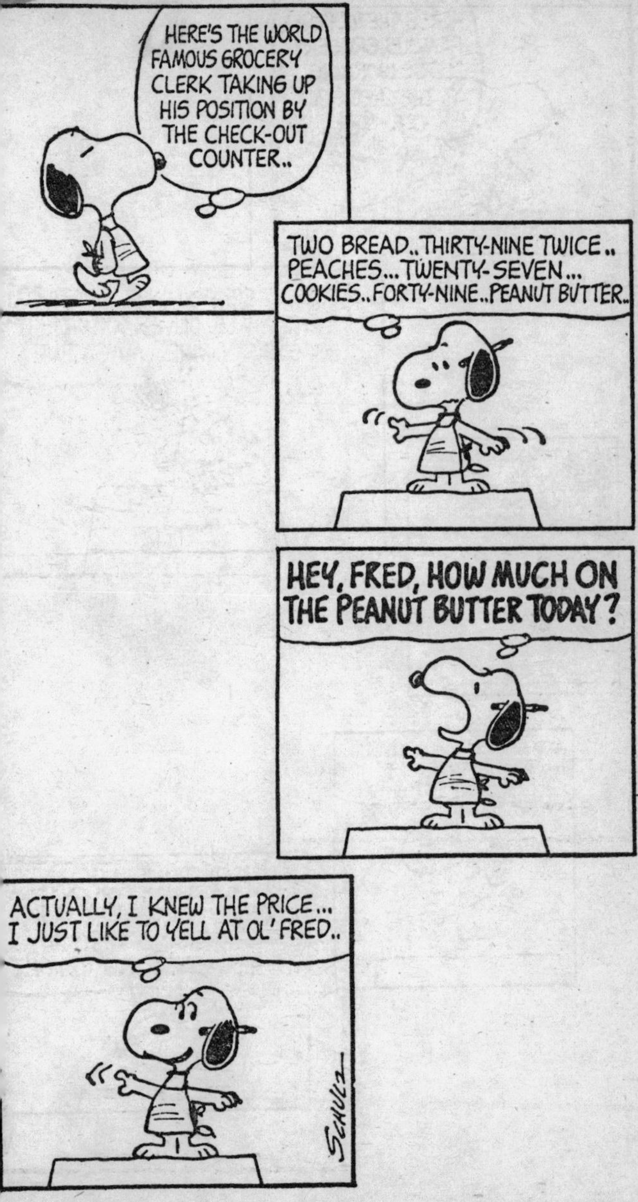
HERE'S THE WORLD FAMOUS GROCERY CLERK TAKING UP HIS POSITION BY THE CHECK-OUT COUNTER..
TWO BREAD.. THIRTY-NINE TWICE.. PEACHES... TWENTY-SEVEN... COOKIES.. FORTY-NINE.. PEANUT BUTTER..
HEY, FRED, HOW MUCH ON THE PEANUT BUTTER TODAY?
ACTUALLY, I KNEW THE PRICE... I JUST LIKE TO YELL AT OL' FRED..
SCHULZ

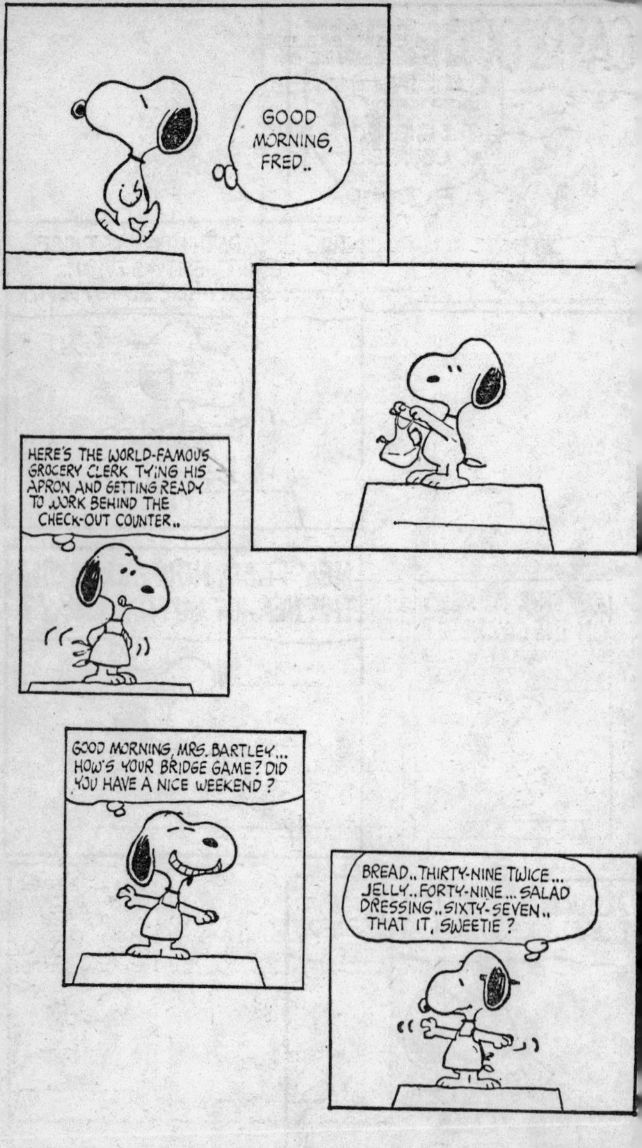
GOOD MORNING, FRED..
HERE'S THE WORLD-FAMOUS GROCERY CLERK TYING HIS APRON AND GETTING READY TO WORK BEHIND THE CHECK-OUT COUNTER..
GOOD MORNING, MRS. BARTLEY... HOW'S YOUR BRIDGE GAME? DID YOU HAVE A NICE WEEKEND?
BREAD.. THIRTY-NINE TWICE... JELLY.. FORTY-NINE... SALAD DRESSING.. SIXTY-SEVEN.. THAT IT, SWEETIE?

CARRY OUT

OH, I'M SORRY, MRS. BARTLEY..I DIDN'T MEAN TO STARTLE YOU..

GOOD MORNING, MRS. LOCKHART.. HOW ARE YOU TODAY? HOW'S ALL THE FAMILY?

PICKLES.. SIXTY.. BREAD.. THIRTY-NINE THRICE..EGGS.. FIFTY-NINE TWICE..CARROTS..

HEY, FRED, HOW MUCH ON THE CARROTS?

DID YOU HAVE ANY BOTTLES, MRS. LOCKHART? THANK YOU

GOOD MORNING, MRS. MENDELSON..HAS YOUR HUSBAND FOUND A JOB YET? HOW WAS YOUR TRIP TO HAWAII?

BREAD..THIRTY-NINE EIGHT TIMES..SOUP.. TWO FOR TWENTY-NINE..TEN CANS... COFFEE... A DOLLAR SEVENTY-EIGHT... TUNA..THIRTY-NINE TWICE..

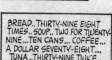

☀ SIGH ☀ SEVEN HOURS AND FORTY MINUTES TO GO... GOOD MORNING, MRS. ALBO..HOW ARE YOU TODAY..SWEETIE?

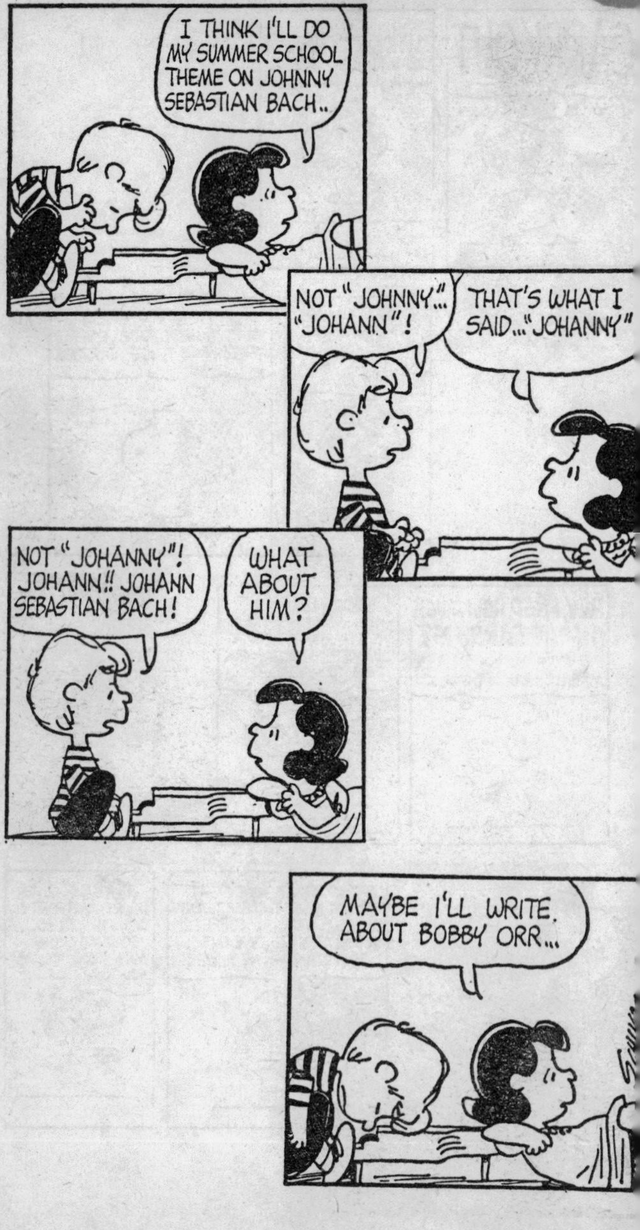
I THINK I'LL DO MY SUMMER SCHOOL THEME ON JOHNNY SEBASTIAN BACH..
NOT "JOHNNY"... "JOHANN"!
THAT'S WHAT I SAID..."JOHANNY"
NOT "JOHANNY"! JOHANN!! JOHANN SEBASTIAN BACH!
WHAT ABOUT HIM?
MAYBE I'LL WRITE ABOUT BOBBY ORR...

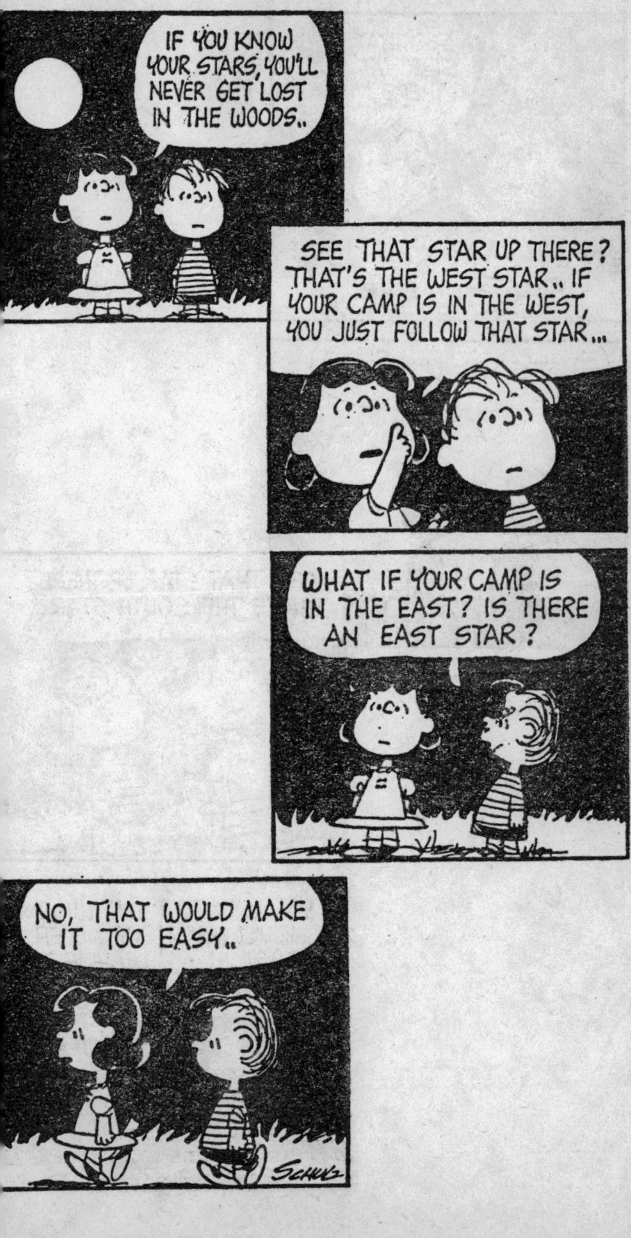
IF YOU KNOW YOUR STARS, YOU'LL NEVER GET LOST IN THE WOODS..
SEE THAT STAR UP THERE? THAT'S THE WEST STAR.. IF YOUR CAMP IS IN THE WEST, YOU JUST FOLLOW THAT STAR...
WHAT IF YOUR CAMP IS IN THE EAST? IS THERE AN EAST STAR?
NO, THAT WOULD MAKE IT TOO EASY..
SCHULZ

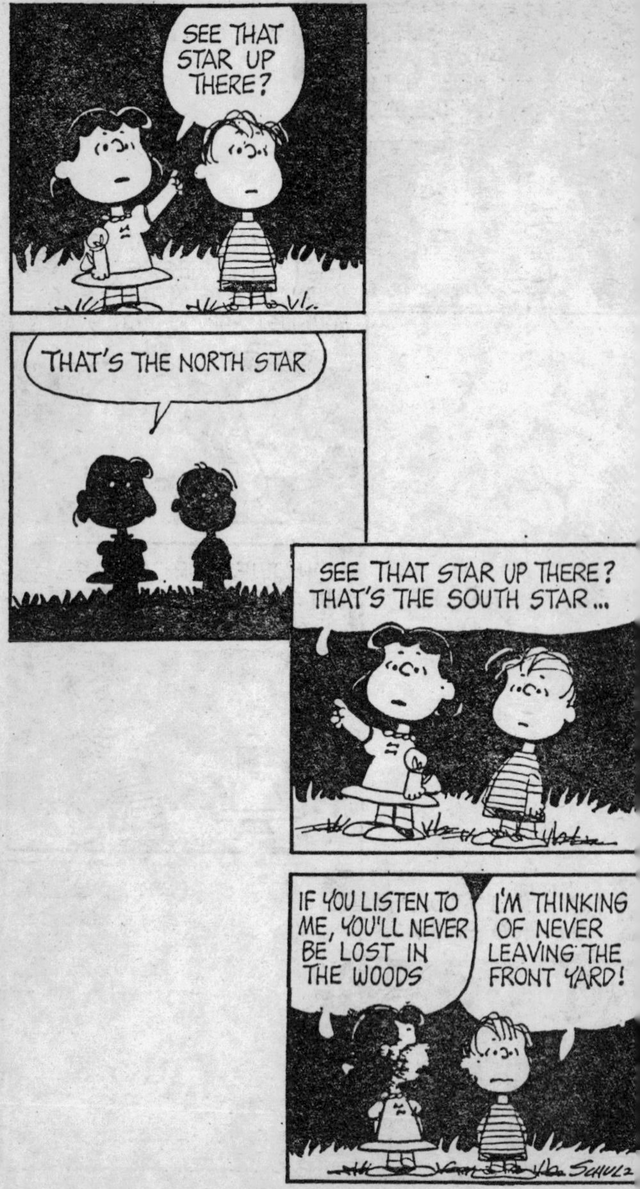
SEE THAT STAR UP THERE?
THAT'S THE NORTH STAR
SEE THAT STAR UP THERE? THAT'S THE SOUTH STAR...
IF YOU LISTEN TO ME, YOU'LL NEVER BE LOST IN THE WOODS
I'M THINKING OF NEVER LEAVING THE FRONT YARD!
SCHULZ

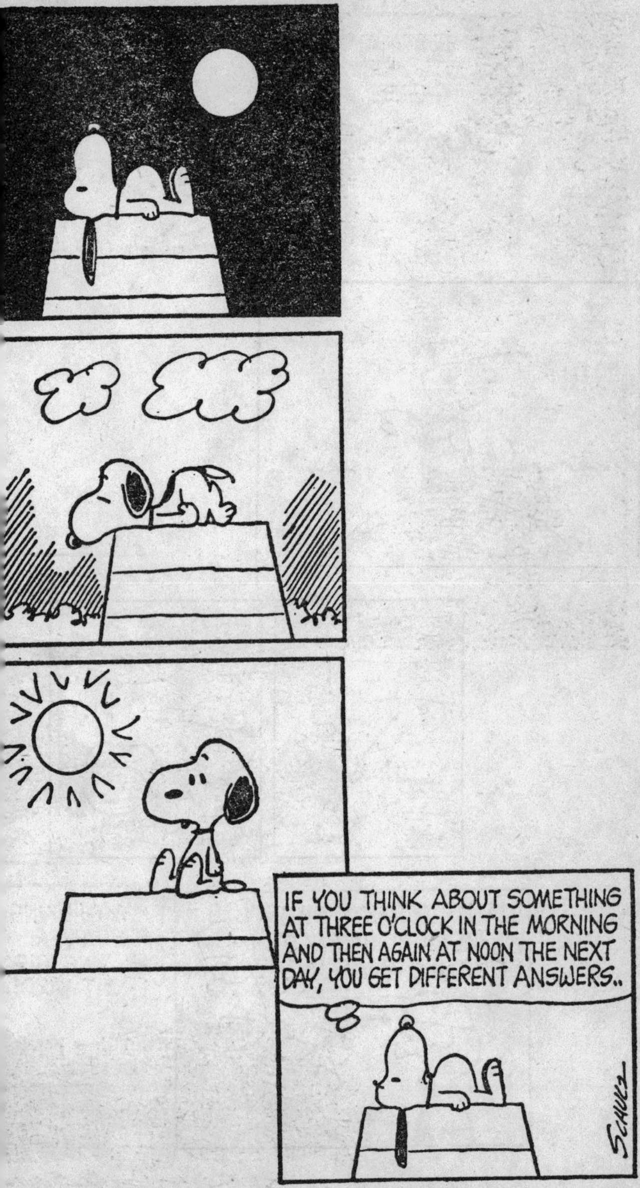
IF YOU THINK ABOUT SOMETHING AT THREE O'CLOCK IN THE MORNING AND THEN AGAIN AT NOON THE NEXT DAY, YOU GET DIFFERENT ANSWERS..
SCHULZ

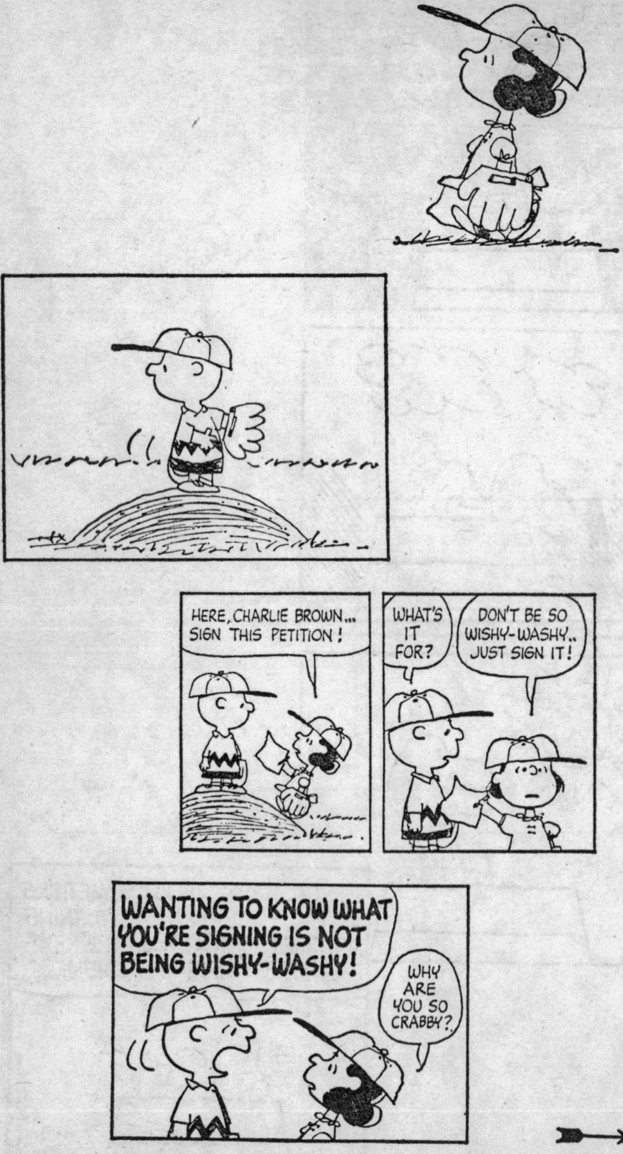
HERE, CHARLIE BROWN... SIGN THIS PETITION!
WHAT'S IT FOR?
DON'T BE SO WISHY-WASHY.. JUST SIGN IT!
WANTING TO KNOW WHAT YOU'RE SIGNING IS NOT BEING WISHY-WASHY!
WHY ARE YOU SO CRABBY?

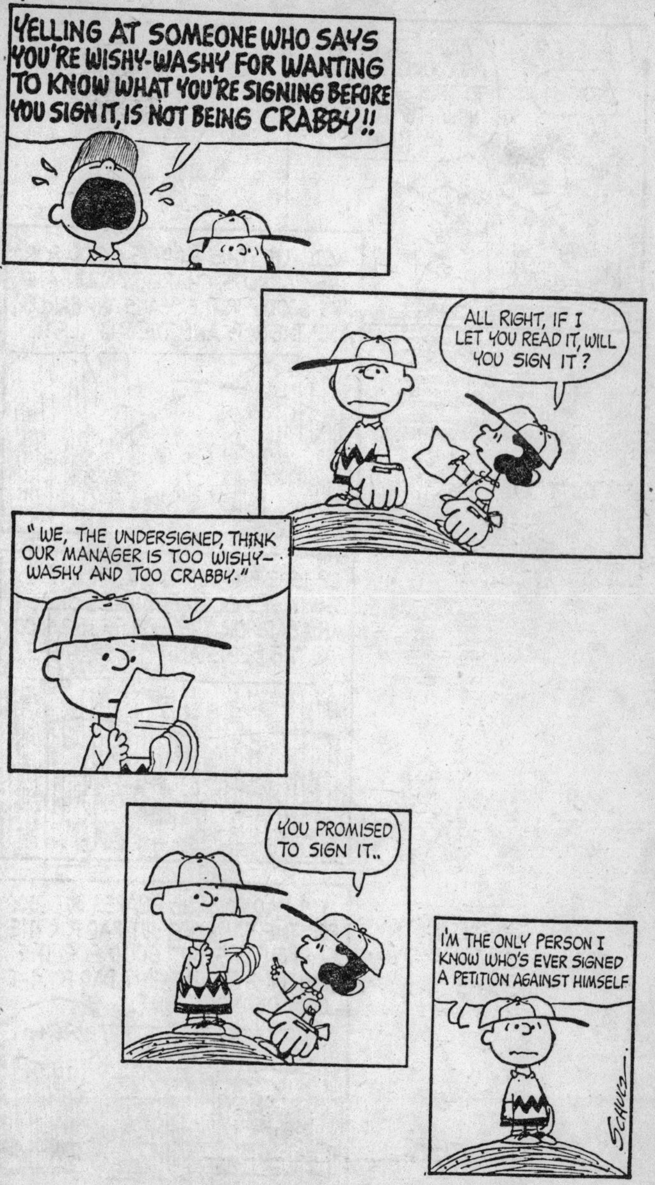
YELLING AT SOMEONE WHO SAYS YOU'RE WISHY-WASHY FOR WANTING TO KNOW WHAT YOU'RE SIGNING BEFORE YOU SIGN IT, IS NOT BEING CRABBY!!
ALL RIGHT, IF I LET YOU READ IT, WILL YOU SIGN IT?
"WE, THE UNDERSIGNED, THINK OUR MANAGER IS TOO WISHY-WASHY AND TOO CRABBY."
YOU PROMISED TO SIGN IT..
I'M THE ONLY PERSON I KNOW WHO'S EVER SIGNED A PETITION AGAINST HIMSELF
SCHULZ

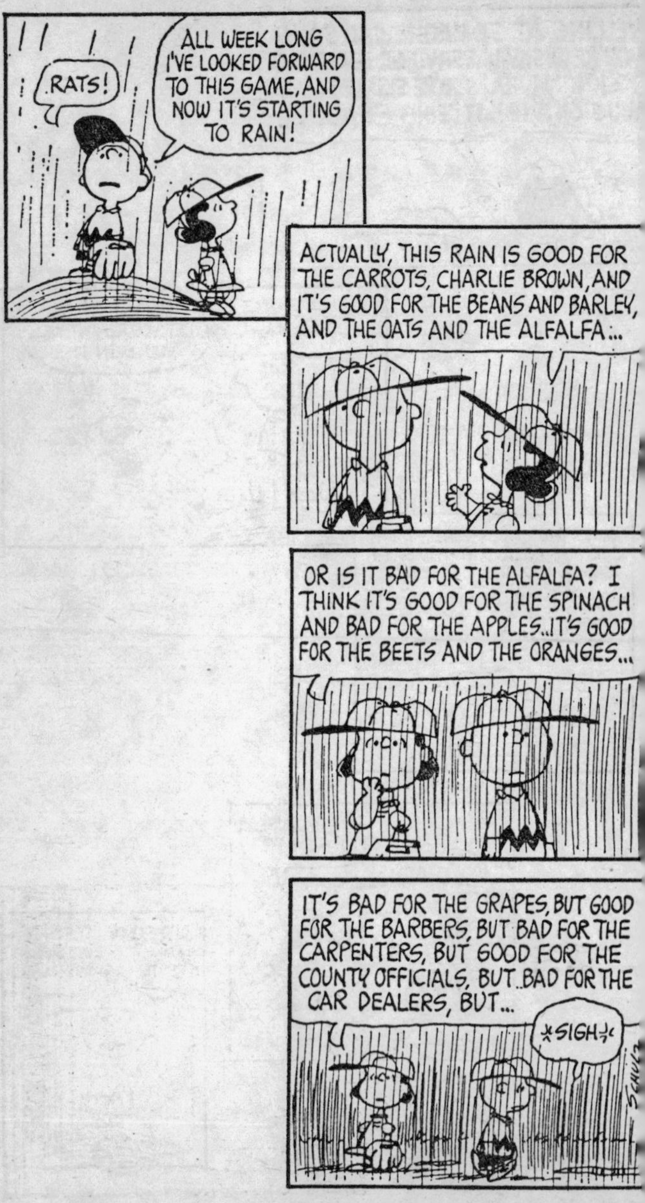
RATS!
ALL WEEK LONG I'VE LOOKED FORWARD TO THIS GAME, AND NOW IT'S STARTING TO RAIN!
ACTUALLY, THIS RAIN IS GOOD FOR THE CARROTS, CHARLIE BROWN, AND IT'S GOOD FOR THE BEANS AND BARLEY, AND THE OATS AND THE ALFALFA...
OR IS IT BAD FOR THE ALFALFA? I THINK IT'S GOOD FOR THE SPINACH AND BAD FOR THE APPLES..IT'S GOOD FOR THE BEETS AND THE ORANGES...
IT'S BAD FOR THE GRAPES, BUT GOOD FOR THE BARBERS, BUT BAD FOR THE CARPENTERS, BUT GOOD FOR THE COUNTY OFFICIALS, BUT..BAD FOR THE CAR DEALERS, BUT...
SIGH
SCHULZ

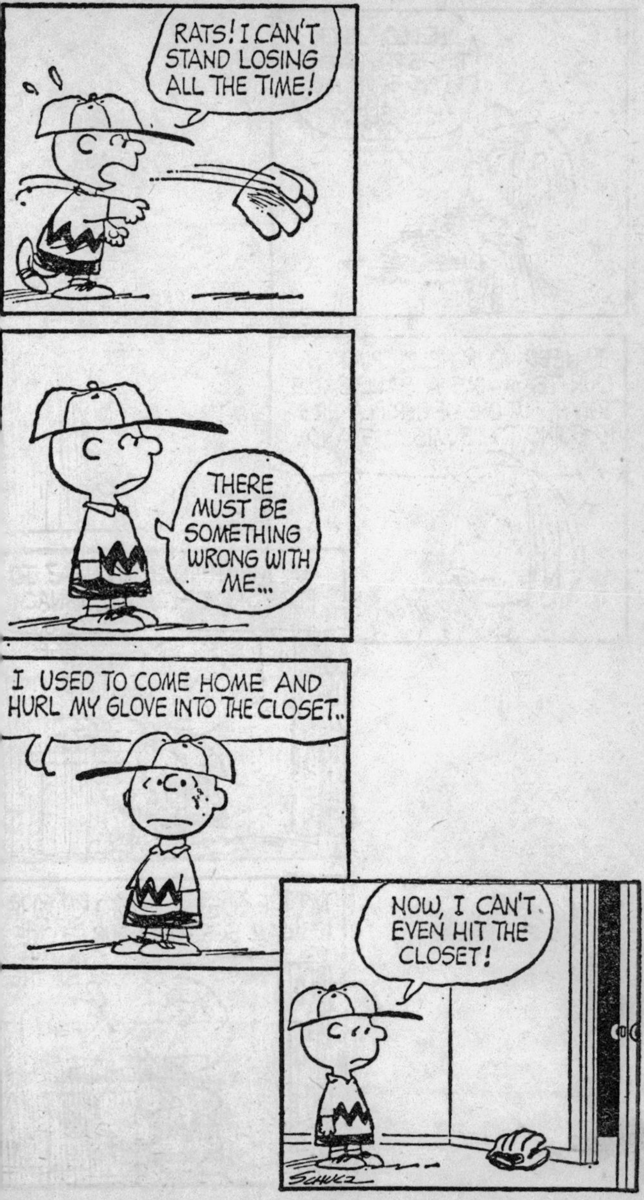
RATS! I CAN'T STAND LOSING ALL THE TIME!
THERE MUST BE SOMETHING WRONG WITH ME...
I USED TO COME HOME AND HURL MY GLOVE INTO THE CLOSET..
NOW, I CAN'T EVEN HIT THE CLOSET!
SCHULZ

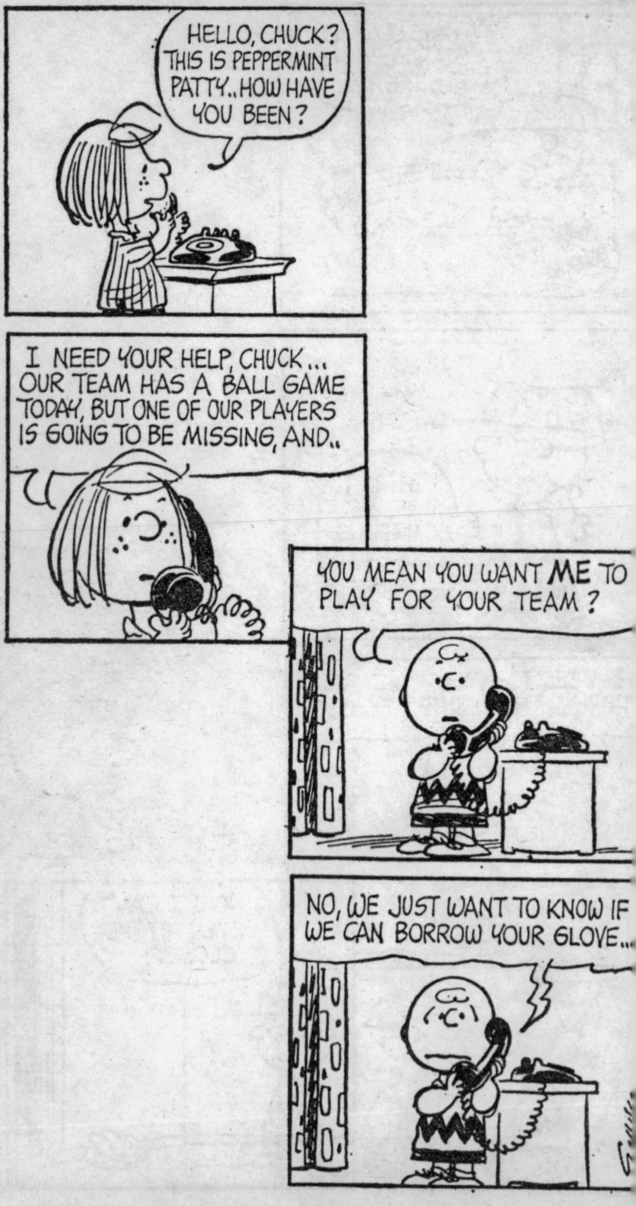

HELLO, CHUCK? THIS IS PEPPERMINT PATTY.. HOW HAVE YOU BEEN?
I NEED YOUR HELP, CHUCK... OUR TEAM HAS A BALL GAME TODAY, BUT ONE OF OUR PLAYERS IS GOING TO BE MISSING, AND..
YOU MEAN YOU WANT ME TO PLAY FOR YOUR TEAM?
NO, WE JUST WANT TO KNOW IF WE CAN BORROW YOUR GLOVE...

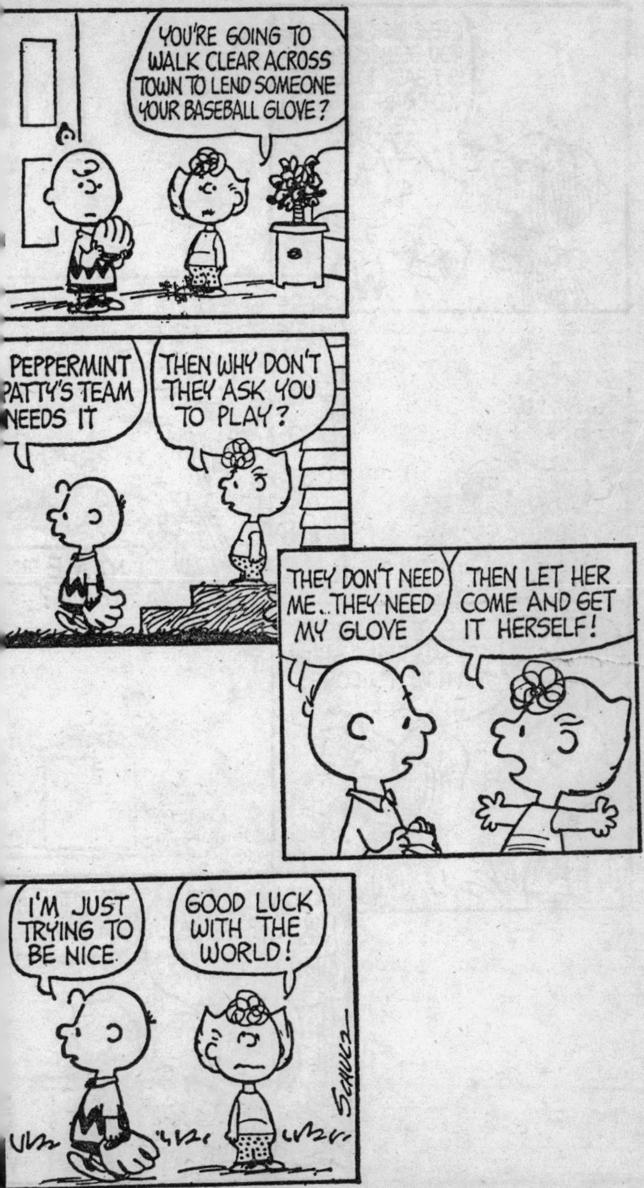
YOU'RE GOING TO WALK CLEAR ACROSS TOWN TO LEND SOMEONE YOUR BASEBALL GLOVE?
PEPPERMINT PATTY'S TEAM NEEDS IT
THEN WHY DON'T THEY ASK YOU TO PLAY?
THEY DON'T NEED ME...THEY NEED MY GLOVE
THEN LET HER COME AND GET IT HERSELF!
I'M JUST TRYING TO BE NICE
GOOD LUCK WITH THE WORLD!
SCHULZ

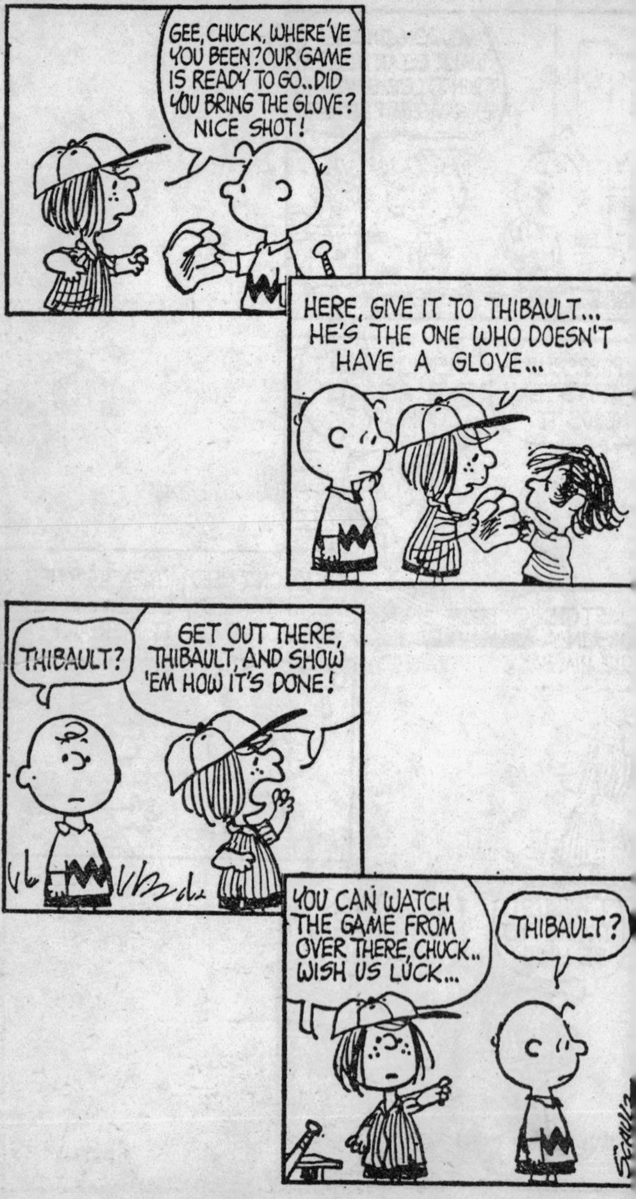
GEE, CHUCK, WHERE'VE YOU BEEN? OUR GAME IS READY TO GO.. DID YOU BRING THE GLOVE? NICE SHOT!
HERE, GIVE IT TO THIBAULT... HE'S THE ONE WHO DOESN'T HAVE A GLOVE...
THIBAULT?
GET OUT THERE, THIBAULT, AND SHOW 'EM HOW IT'S DONE!
YOU CAN WATCH THE GAME FROM OVER THERE, CHUCK.. WISH US LUCK...
THIBAULT?

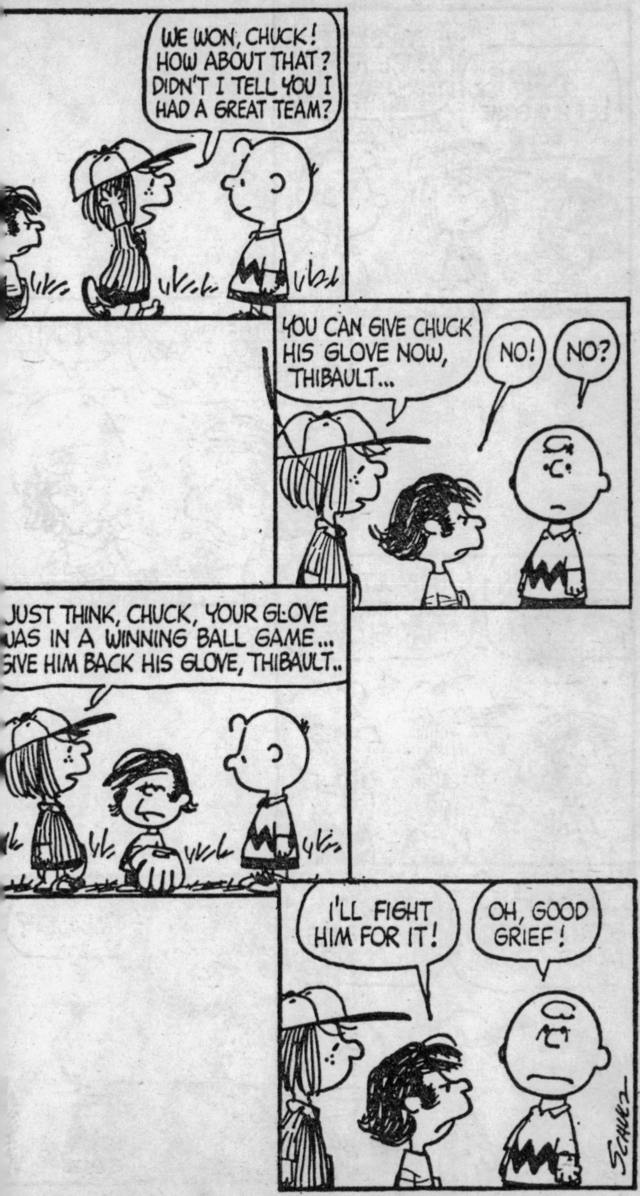
WE WON, CHUCK! HOW ABOUT THAT? DIDN'T I TELL YOU I HAD A GREAT TEAM?
YOU CAN GIVE CHUCK HIS GLOVE NOW, THIBAULT...
NO!
NO?
JUST THINK, CHUCK, YOUR GLOVE WAS IN A WINNING BALL GAME... GIVE HIM BACK HIS GLOVE, THIBAULT..
I'LL FIGHT HIM FOR IT!
OH, GOOD GRIEF!
SCHULZ

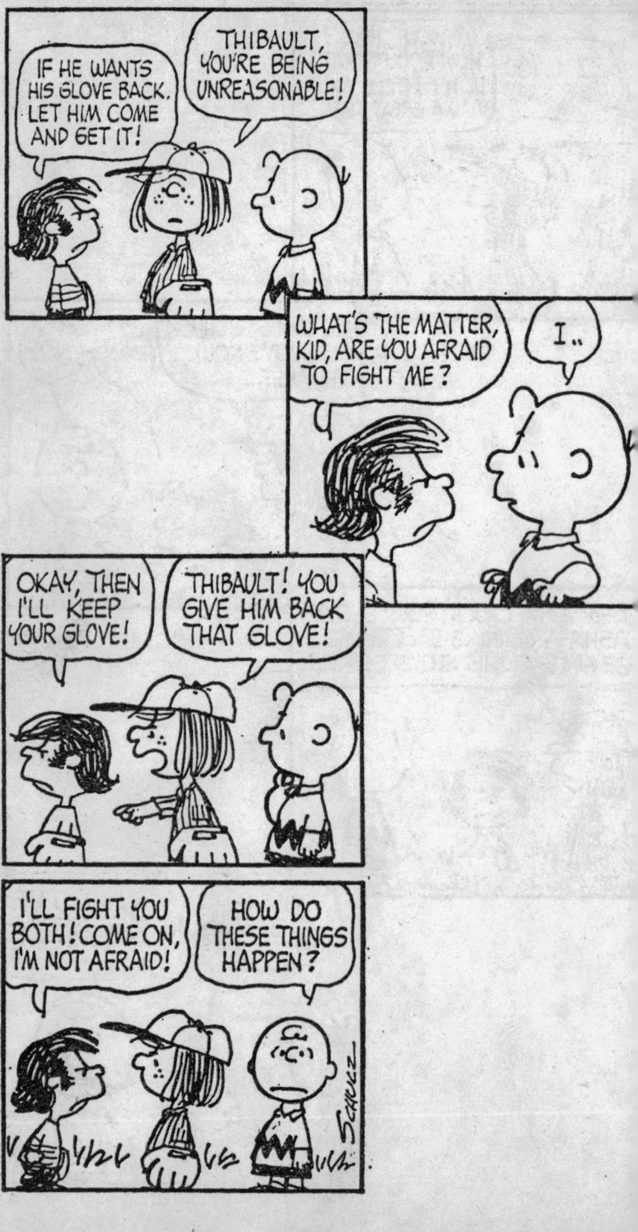
IF HE WANTS HIS GLOVE BACK. LET HIM COME AND GET IT!
THIBAULT, YOU'RE BEING UNREASONABLE!
WHAT'S THE MATTER, KID, ARE YOU AFRAID TO FIGHT ME?
I..
OKAY, THEN I'LL KEEP YOUR GLOVE!
THIBAULT! YOU GIVE HIM BACK THAT GLOVE!
I'LL FIGHT YOU BOTH! COME ON, I'M NOT AFRAID!
HOW DO THESE THINGS HAPPEN?
SCHULZ

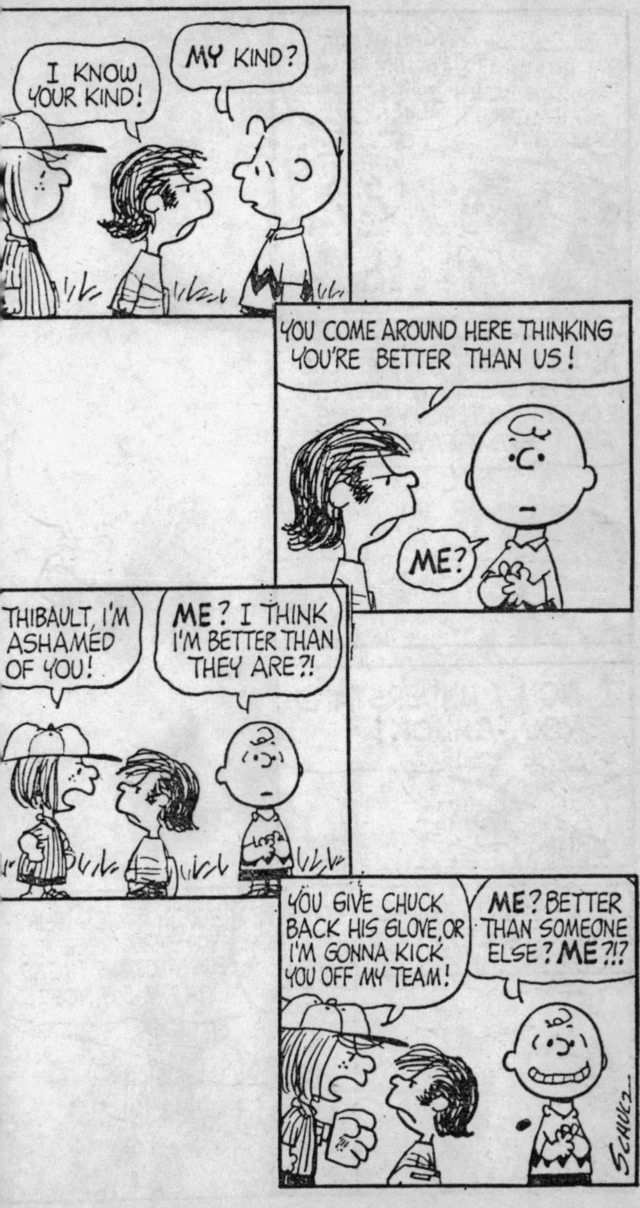
I KNOW YOUR KIND!
MY KIND?
YOU COME AROUND HERE THINKING YOU'RE BETTER THAN US!
ME?
THIBAULT, I'M ASHAMED OF YOU!
ME? I THINK I'M BETTER THAN THEY ARE?!
YOU GIVE CHUCK BACK HIS GLOVE, OR I'M GONNA KICK YOU OFF MY TEAM!
ME? BETTER THAN SOMEONE ELSE? ME?!?
SCHULZ

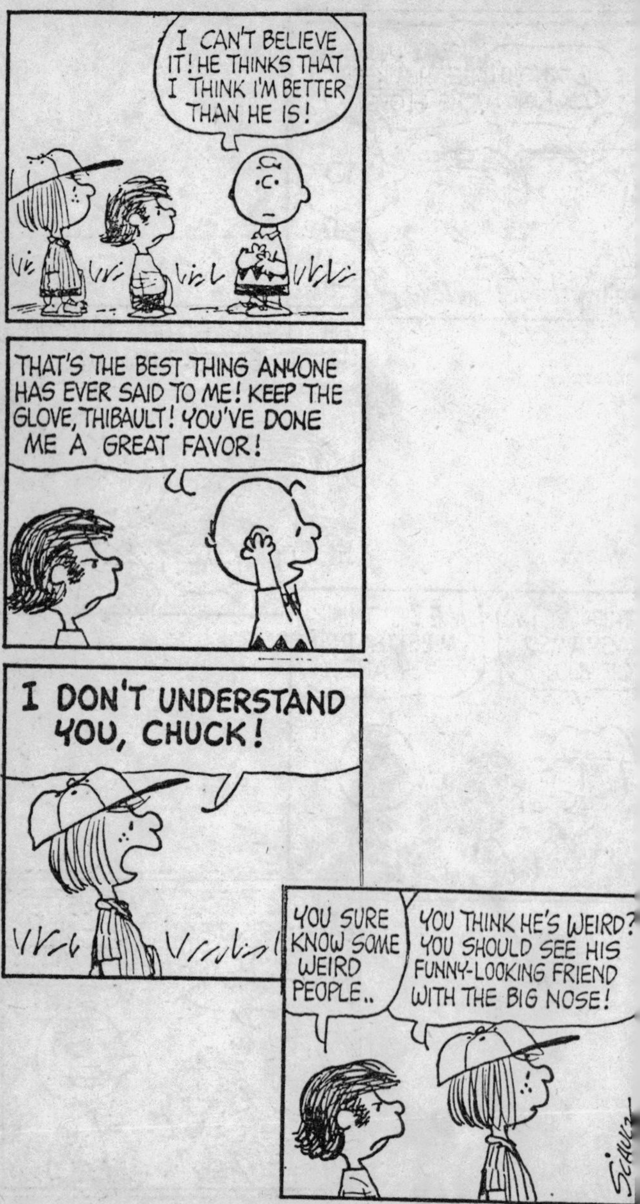
I CAN'T BELIEVE IT! HE THINKS THAT I THINK I'M BETTER THAN HE IS!
THAT'S THE BEST THING ANYONE HAS EVER SAID TO ME! KEEP THE GLOVE, THIBAULT! YOU'VE DONE ME A GREAT FAVOR!
I DON'T UNDERSTAND YOU, CHUCK!
YOU SURE KNOW SOME WEIRD PEOPLE..
YOU THINK HE'S WEIRD? YOU SHOULD SEE HIS FUNNY-LOOKING FRIEND WITH THE BIG NOSE!
SCHULZ

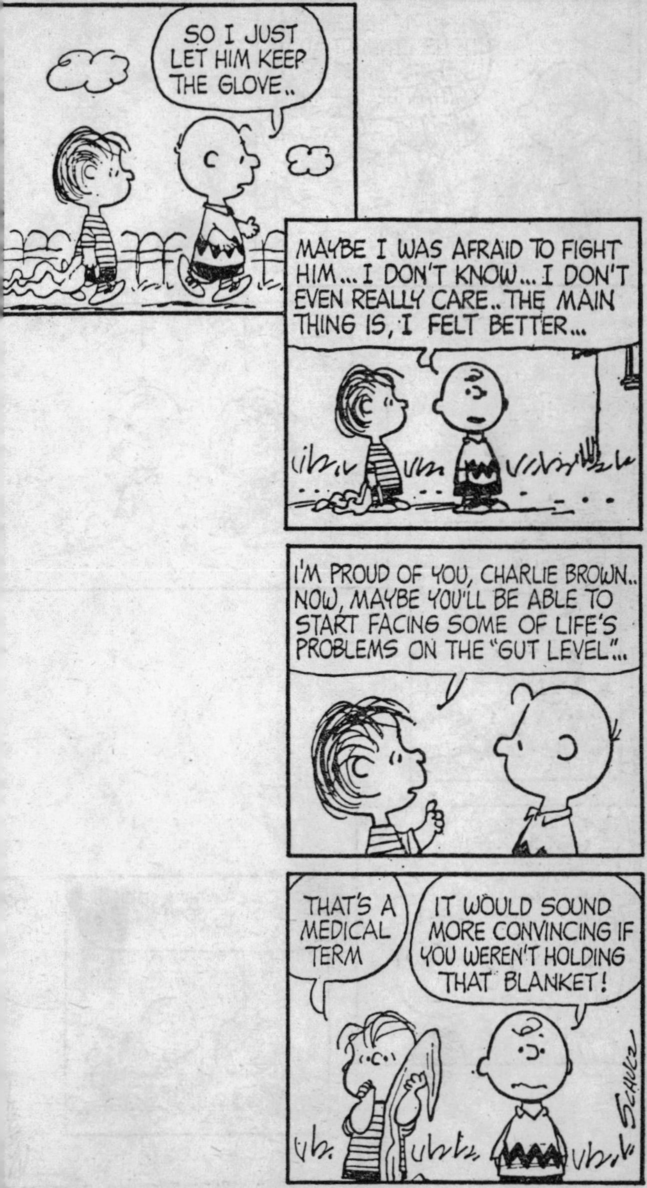
SO I JUST LET HIM KEEP THE GLOVE..
MAYBE I WAS AFRAID TO FIGHT HIM... I DON'T KNOW... I DON'T EVEN REALLY CARE.. THE MAIN THING IS, I FELT BETTER...
I'M PROUD OF YOU, CHARLIE BROWN.. NOW, MAYBE YOU'LL BE ABLE TO START FACING SOME OF LIFE'S PROBLEMS ON THE "GUT LEVEL"...
THAT'S A MEDICAL TERM
IT WOULD SOUND MORE CONVINCING IF YOU WEREN'T HOLDING THAT BLANKET!
SCHULZ

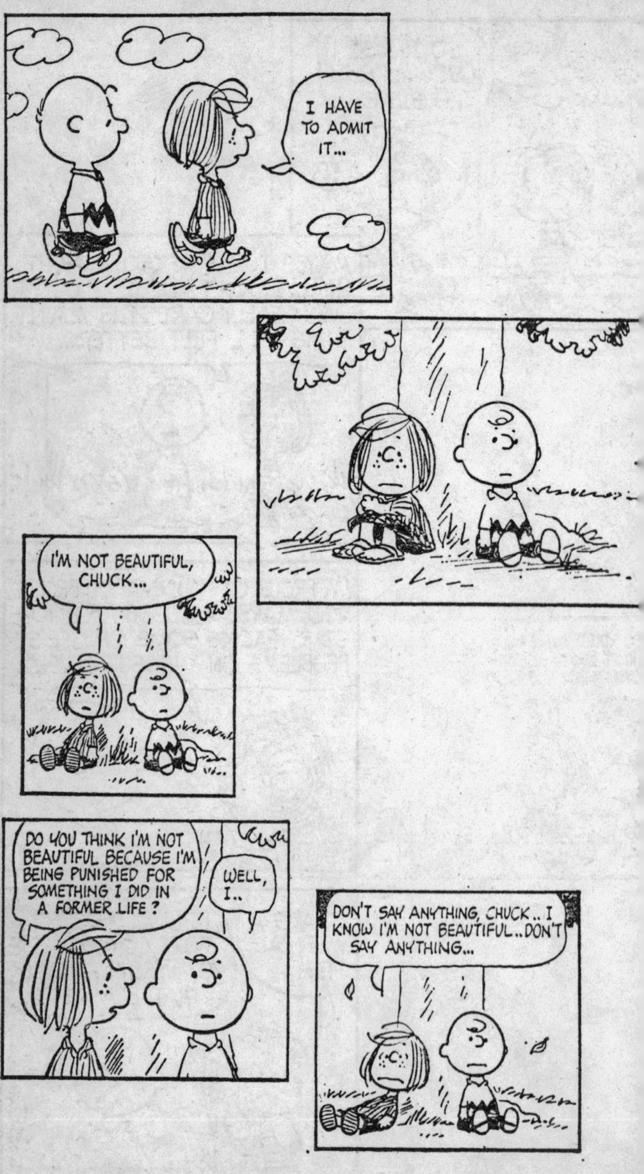

I HAVE TO ADMIT IT...
I'M NOT BEAUTIFUL, CHUCK...
DO YOU THINK I'M NOT BEAUTIFUL BECAUSE I'M BEING PUNISHED FOR SOMETHING I DID IN A FORMER LIFE ?
WELL, I..
DON'T SAY ANYTHING, CHUCK.. I KNOW I'M NOT BEAUTIFUL..DON'T SAY ANYTHING...

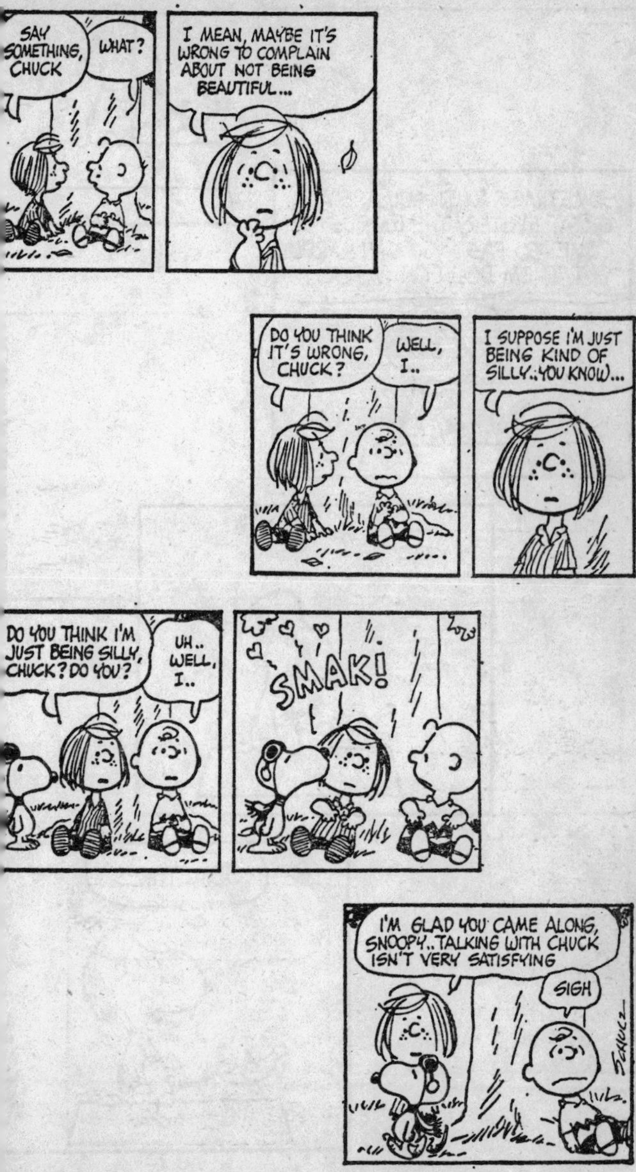
SAY SOMETHING, CHUCK
WHAT?
I MEAN, MAYBE IT'S WRONG TO COMPLAIN ABOUT NOT BEING BEAUTIFUL...
DO YOU THINK IT'S WRONG, CHUCK?
WELL, I..
I SUPPOSE I'M JUST BEING KIND OF SILLY..YOU KNOW...
DO YOU THINK I'M JUST BEING SILLY, CHUCK? DO YOU?
UH.. WELL, I..
SMAK!
I'M GLAD YOU CAME ALONG, SNOOPY..TALKING WITH CHUCK ISN'T VERY SATISFYING
SIGH
SCHULZ

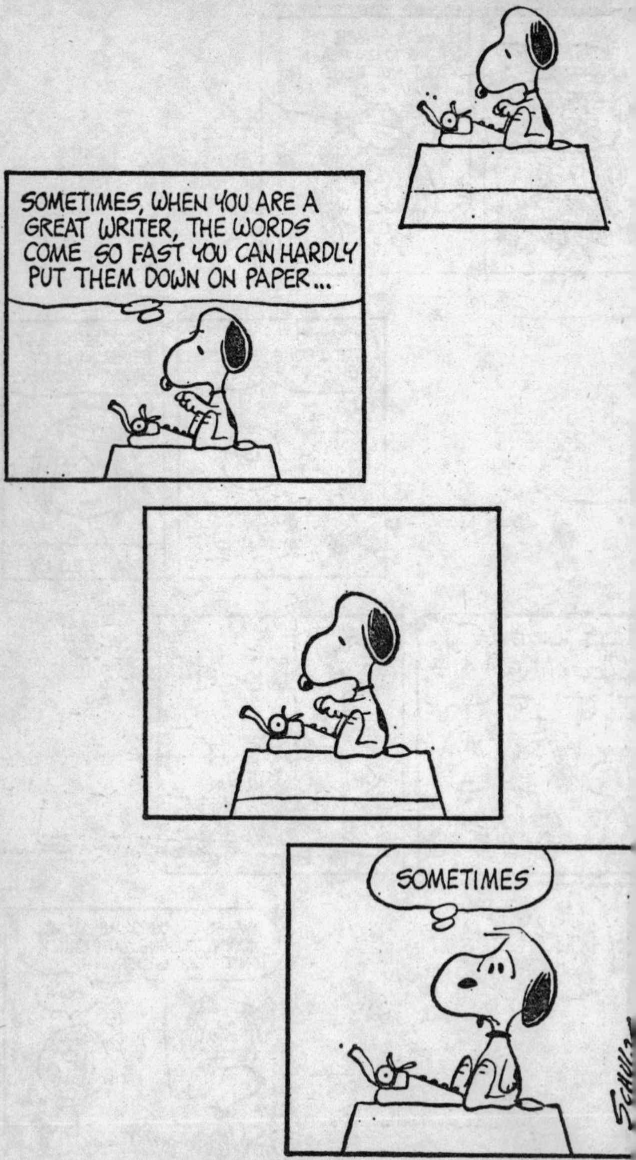
SOMETIMES, WHEN YOU ARE A GREAT WRITER, THE WORDS COME SO FAST YOU CAN HARDLY PUT THEM DOWN ON PAPER...
SOMETIMES

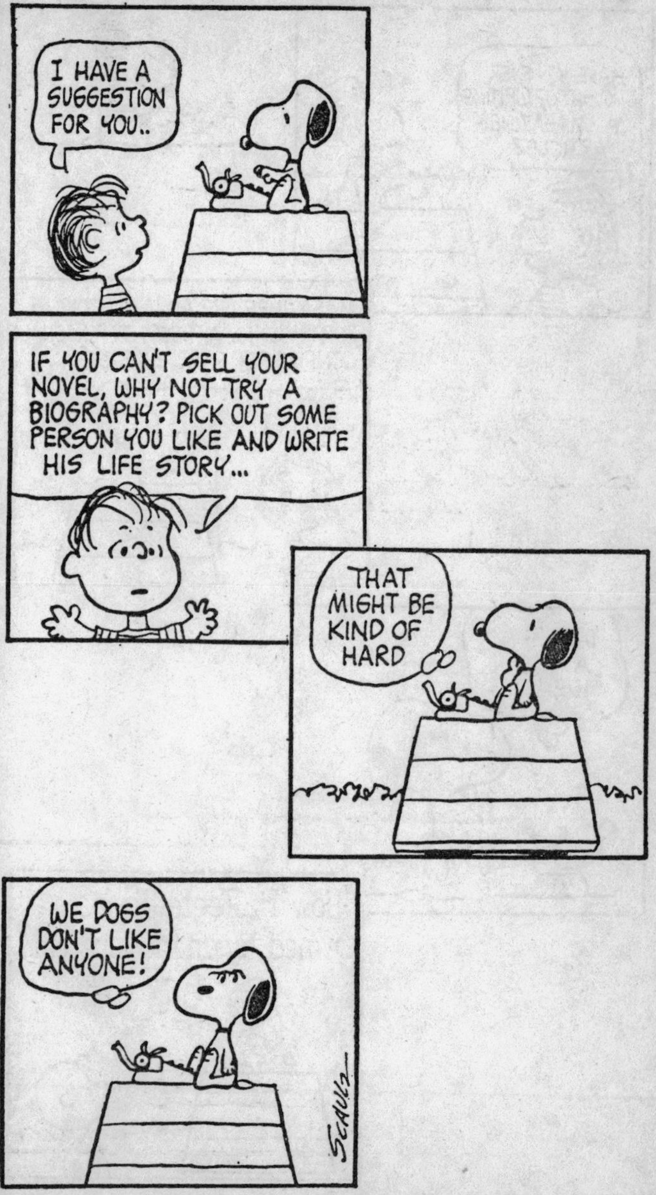
I HAVE A SUGGESTION FOR YOU..
IF YOU CAN'T SELL YOUR NOVEL, WHY NOT TRY A BIOGRAPHY? PICK OUT SOME PERSON YOU LIKE AND WRITE HIS LIFE STORY...
THAT MIGHT BE KIND OF HARD
WE DOGS DON'T LIKE ANYONE!
SCHULZ

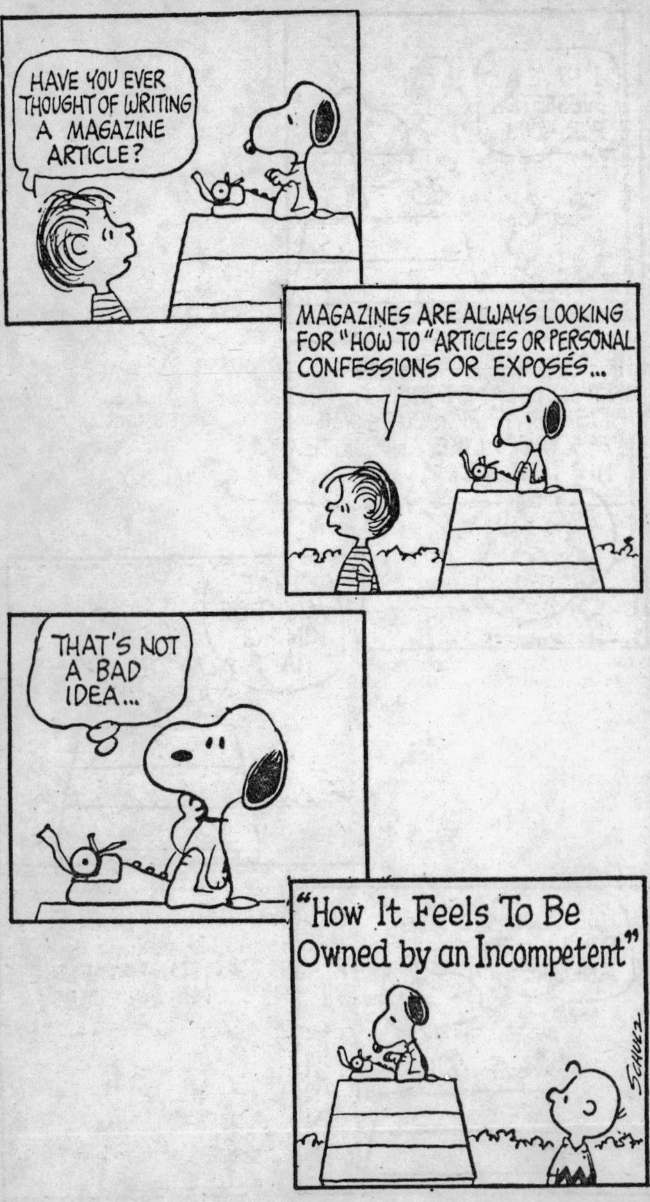
HAVE YOU EVER THOUGHT OF WRITING A MAGAZINE ARTICLE?
MAGAZINES ARE ALWAYS LOOKING FOR "HOW TO" ARTICLES OR PERSONAL CONFESSIONS OR EXPOSÉS...
THAT'S NOT A BAD IDEA...
"How It Feels To Be Owned by an Incompetent"
SCHULZ

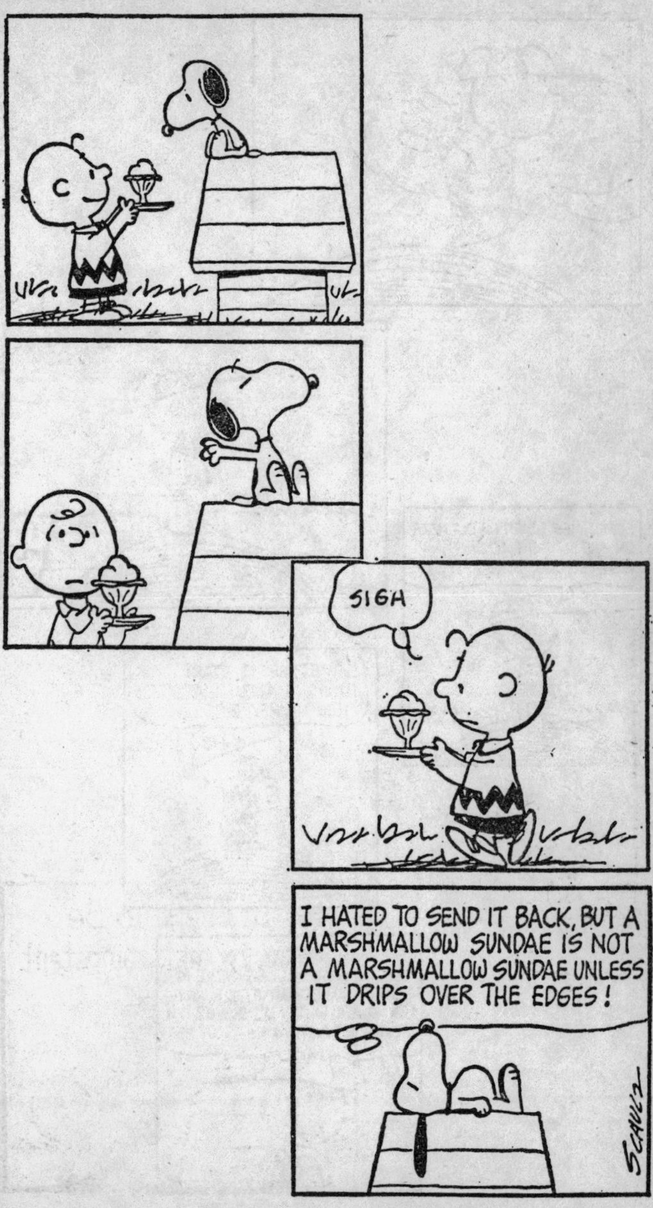
SIGH
I HATED TO SEND IT BACK, BUT A MARSHMALLOW SUNDAE IS NOT A MARSHMALLOW SUNDAE UNLESS IT DRIPS OVER THE EDGES!
SCHULZ

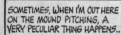

SOMETIMES, WHEN I'M OUT HERE ON THE MOUND PITCHING, A VERY PECULIAR THING HAPPENS..

SOMETIMES I START THINKING ABOUT THAT LITTLE RED-HAIRED GIRL..

HERE I AM, SURROUNDED BY KIDS PLAYING BASEBALL..EVERYONE IS YELLING AND SCREAMING AND RUNNING AROUND, AND WHAT AM I DOING? I'M PITCHING, BUT I'M THINKING ABOUT HER

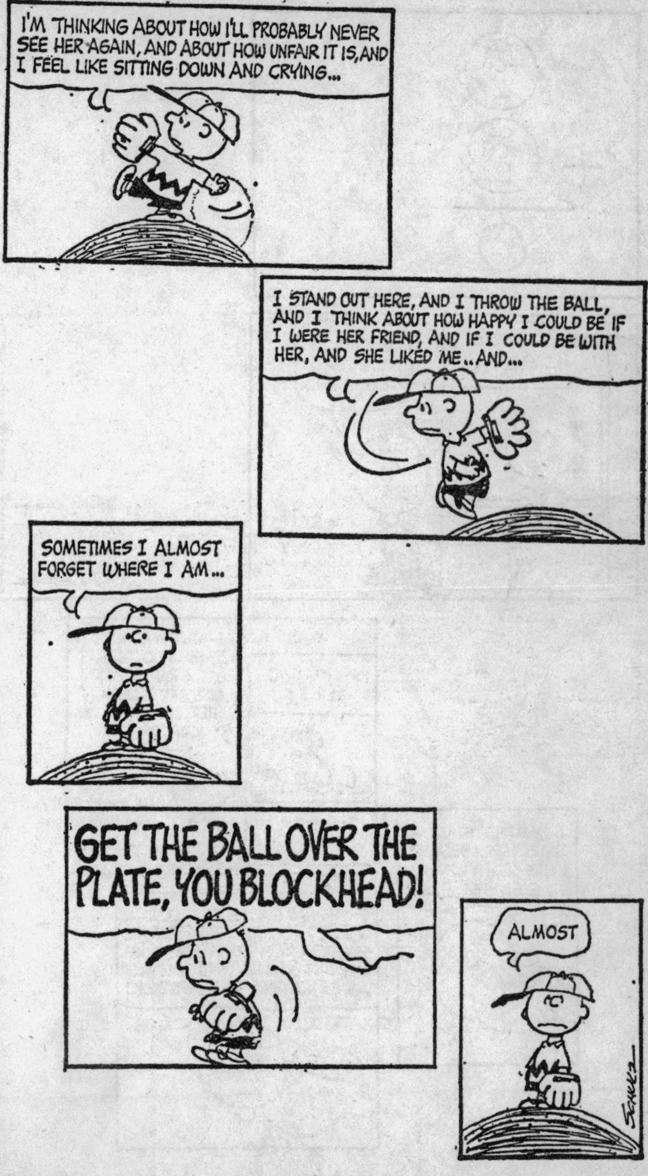

I'M THINKING ABOUT HOW I'LL PROBABLY NEVER SEE HER AGAIN, AND ABOUT HOW UNFAIR IT IS, AND I FEEL LIKE SITTING DOWN AND CRYING...
I STAND OUT HERE, AND I THROW THE BALL, AND I THINK ABOUT HOW HAPPY I COULD BE IF I WERE HER FRIEND, AND IF I COULD BE WITH HER, AND SHE LIKED ME.. AND...
SOMETIMES I ALMOST FORGET WHERE I AM...
GET THE BALL OVER THE PLATE, YOU BLOCKHEAD!
ALMOST
SCHULZ

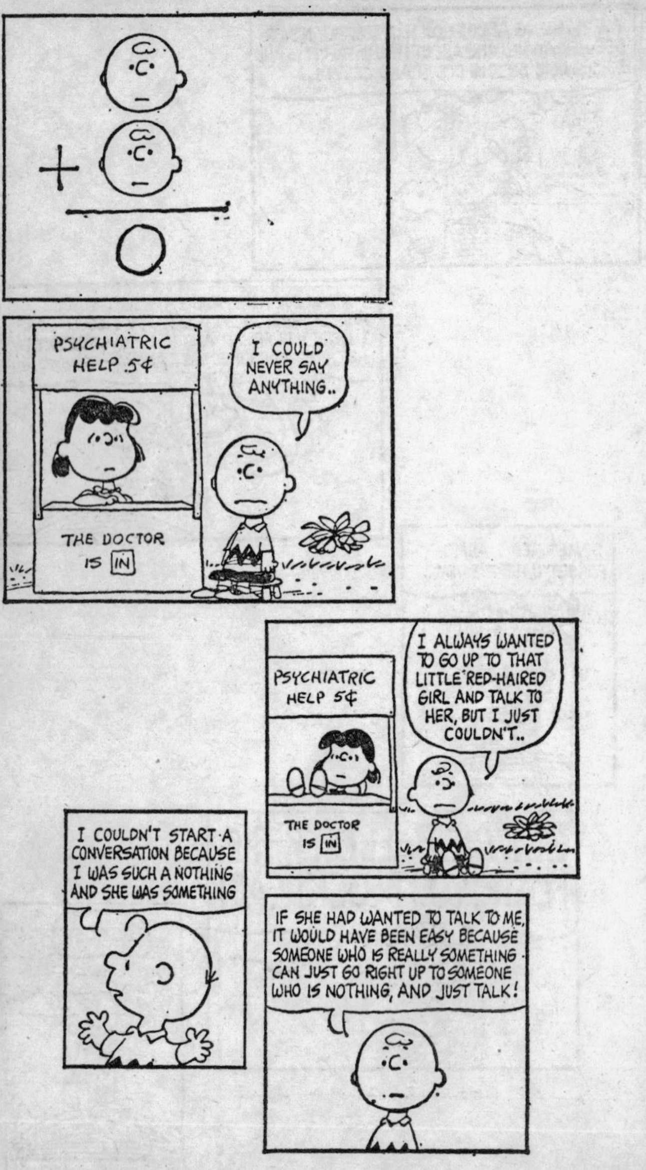
PSYCHIATRIC HELP 5¢
I COULD NEVER SAY ANYTHING..
THE DOCTOR IS IN
PSYCHIATRIC HELP 5¢
I ALWAYS WANTED TO GO UP TO THAT LITTLE RED-HAIRED GIRL AND TALK TO HER, BUT I JUST COULDN'T..
THE DOCTOR IS IN
I COULDN'T START A CONVERSATION BECAUSE I WAS SUCH A NOTHING AND SHE WAS SOMETHING
IF SHE HAD WANTED TO TALK TO ME, IT WOULD HAVE BEEN EASY BECAUSE SOMEONE WHO IS REALLY SOMETHING CAN JUST GO RIGHT UP TO SOMEONE WHO IS NOTHING, AND JUST TALK!

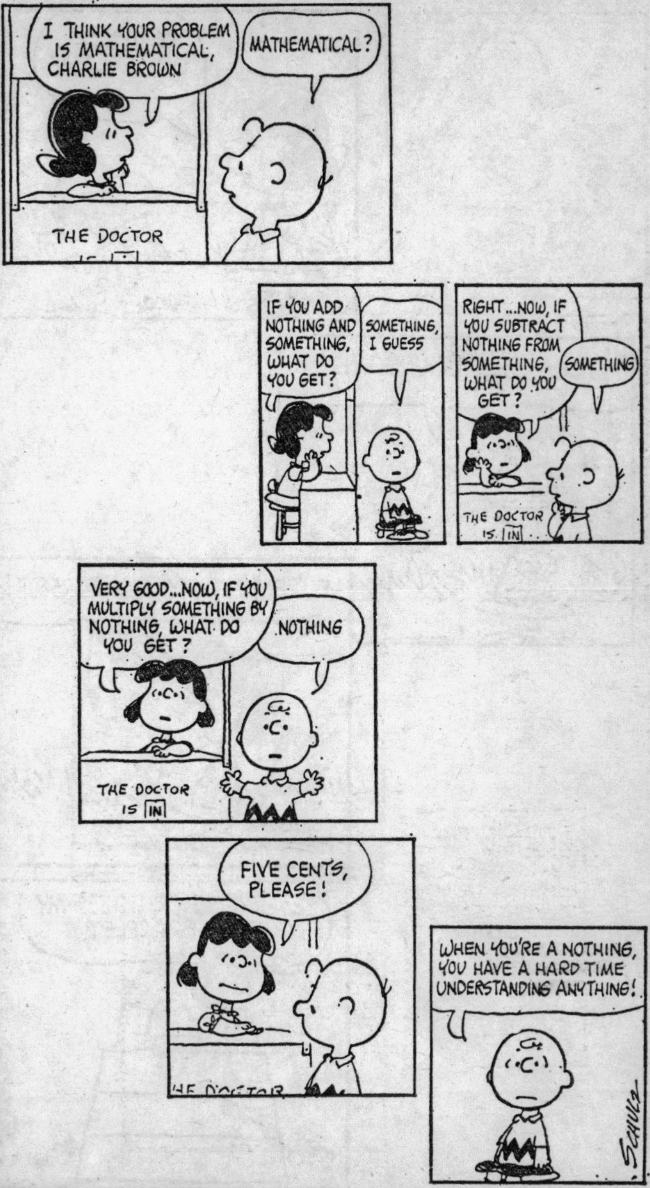
I THINK YOUR PROBLEM IS MATHEMATICAL, CHARLIE BROWN
MATHEMATICAL?
THE DOCTOR
IF YOU ADD NOTHING AND SOMETHING, WHAT DO YOU GET?
SOMETHING, I GUESS
RIGHT...NOW, IF YOU SUBTRACT NOTHING FROM SOMETHING, WHAT DO YOU GET?
SOMETHING
THE DOCTOR IS IN
VERY GOOD...NOW, IF YOU MULTIPLY SOMETHING BY NOTHING, WHAT DO YOU GET?
NOTHING
THE DOCTOR IS IN
FIVE CENTS, PLEASE!
WHEN YOU'RE A NOTHING, YOU HAVE A HARD TIME UNDERSTANDING ANYTHING!
SCHULZ

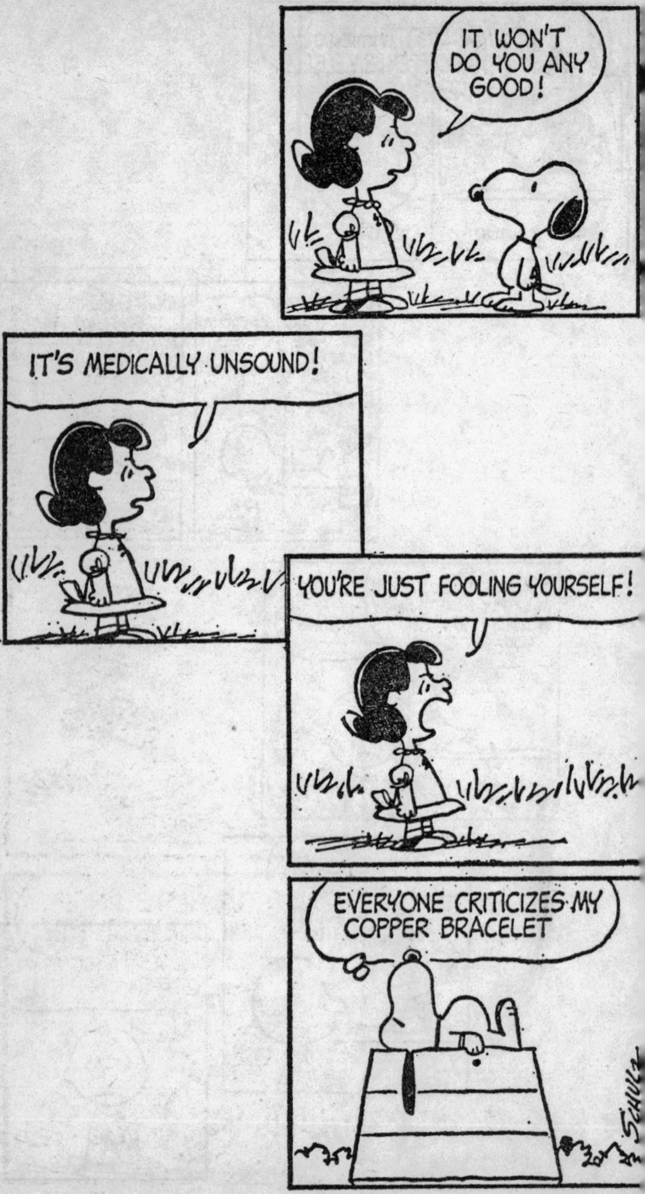
IT WON'T DO YOU ANY GOOD!
IT'S MEDICALLY UNSOUND!
YOU'RE JUST FOOLING YOURSELF!
EVERYONE CRITICIZES MY COPPER BRACELET
SCHULZ

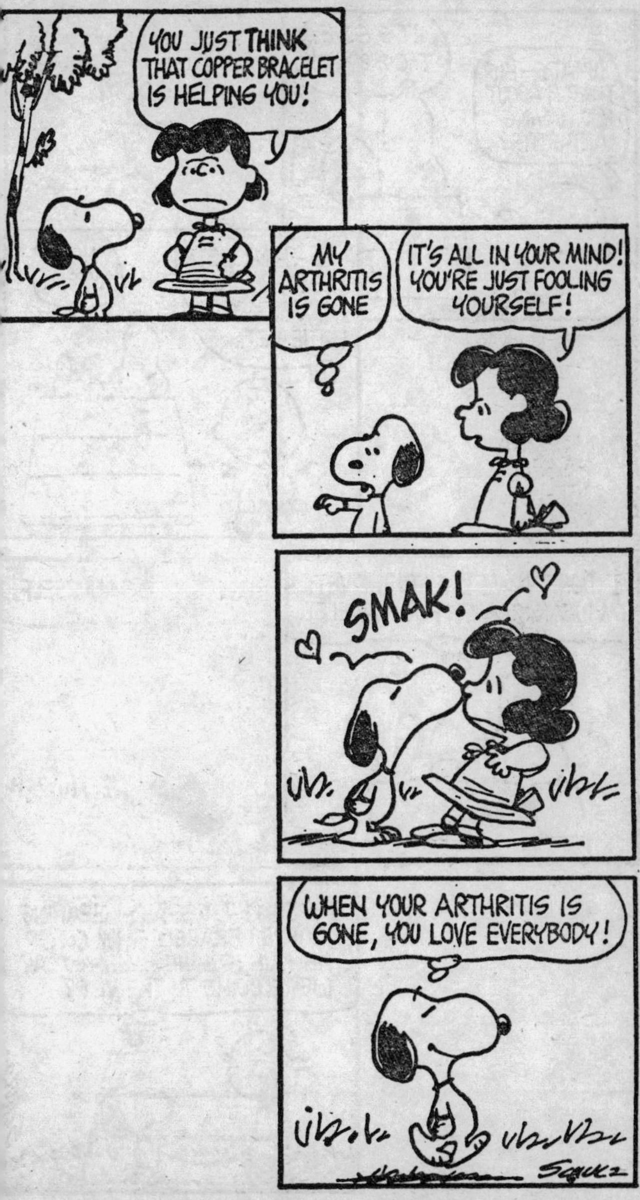
YOU JUST THINK THAT COPPER BRACELET IS HELPING YOU!
MY ARTHRITIS IS GONE
IT'S ALL IN YOUR MIND! YOU'RE JUST FOOLING YOURSELF!
SMAK!
WHEN YOUR ARTHRITIS IS GONE, YOU LOVE EVERYBODY!
SCHULZ

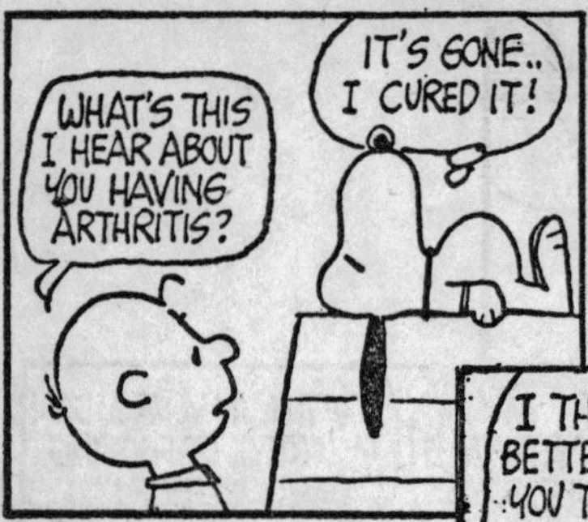
WHAT'S THIS I HEAR ABOUT YOU HAVING ARTHRITIS?
IT'S GONE.. I CURED IT!

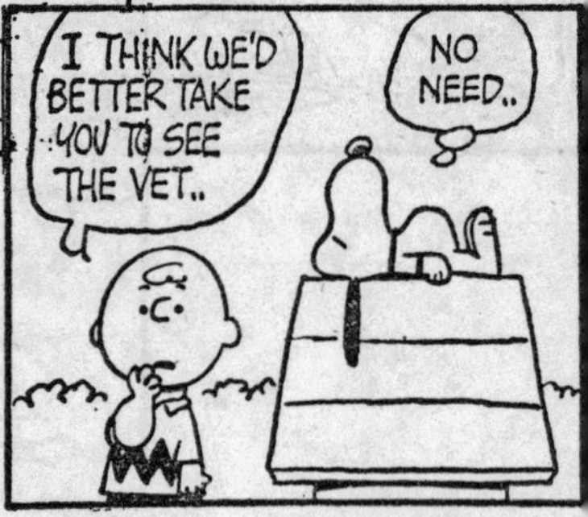
I THINK WE'D BETTER TAKE YOU TO SEE THE VET..
NO NEED..

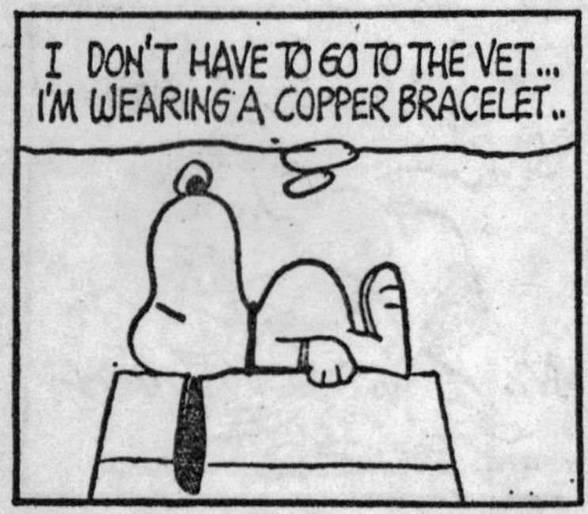
I DON'T HAVE TO GO TO THE VET... I'M WEARING A COPPER BRACELET..

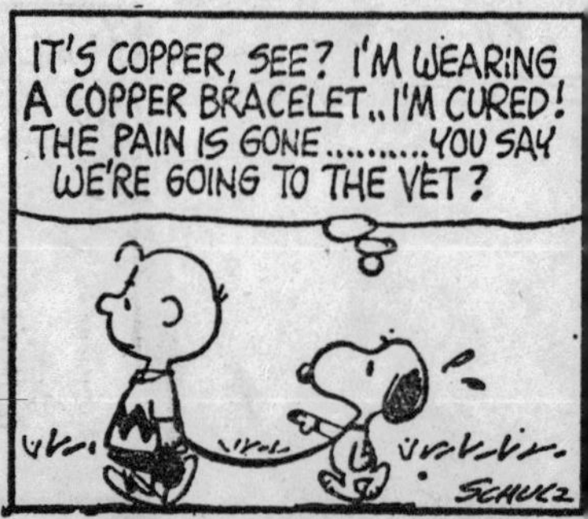
IT'S COPPER, SEE? I'M WEARING A COPPER BRACELET.. I'M CURED! THE PAIN IS GONE..........YOU SAY WE'RE GOING TO THE VET?
SCHULZ

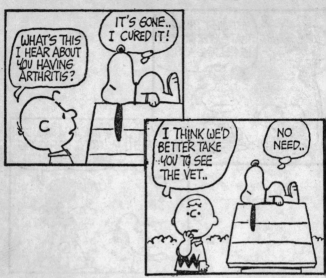

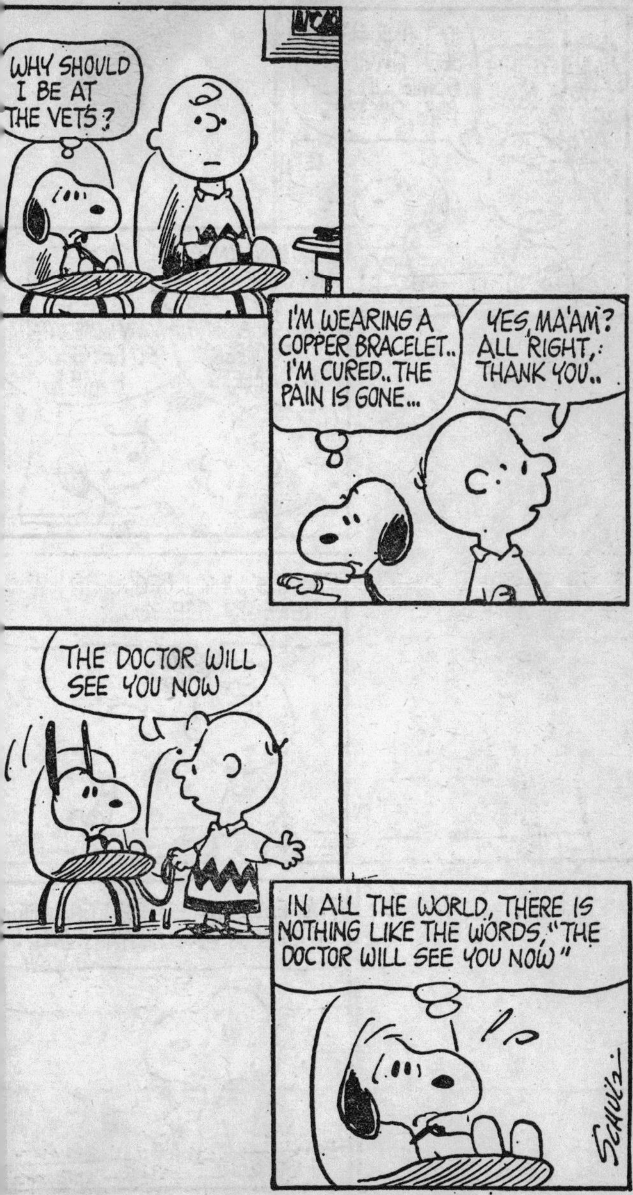
WHY SHOULD I BE AT THE VET'S ?
I'M WEARING A COPPER BRACELET.. I'M CURED.. THE PAIN IS GONE...
YES, MA'AM? ALL RIGHT, THANK YOU..
THE DOCTOR WILL SEE YOU NOW
IN ALL THE WORLD, THERE IS NOTHING LIKE THE WORDS, "THE DOCTOR WILL SEE YOU NOW"
SCHULZ

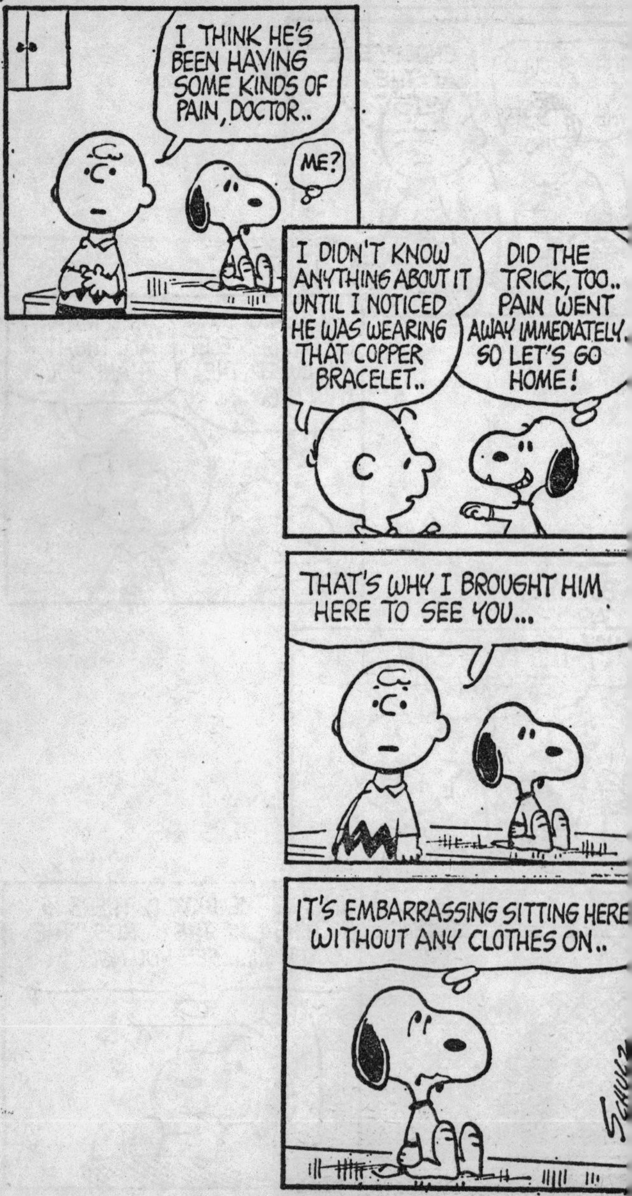
I THINK HE'S BEEN HAVING SOME KINDS OF PAIN, DOCTOR..
ME?
I DIDN'T KNOW ANYTHING ABOUT IT UNTIL I NOTICED HE WAS WEARING THAT COPPER BRACELET..
DID THE TRICK, TOO.. PAIN WENT AWAY IMMEDIATELY. SO LET'S GO HOME!
THAT'S WHY I BROUGHT HIM HERE TO SEE YOU...
IT'S EMBARRASSING SITTING HERE WITHOUT ANY CLOTHES ON..
SCHULZ

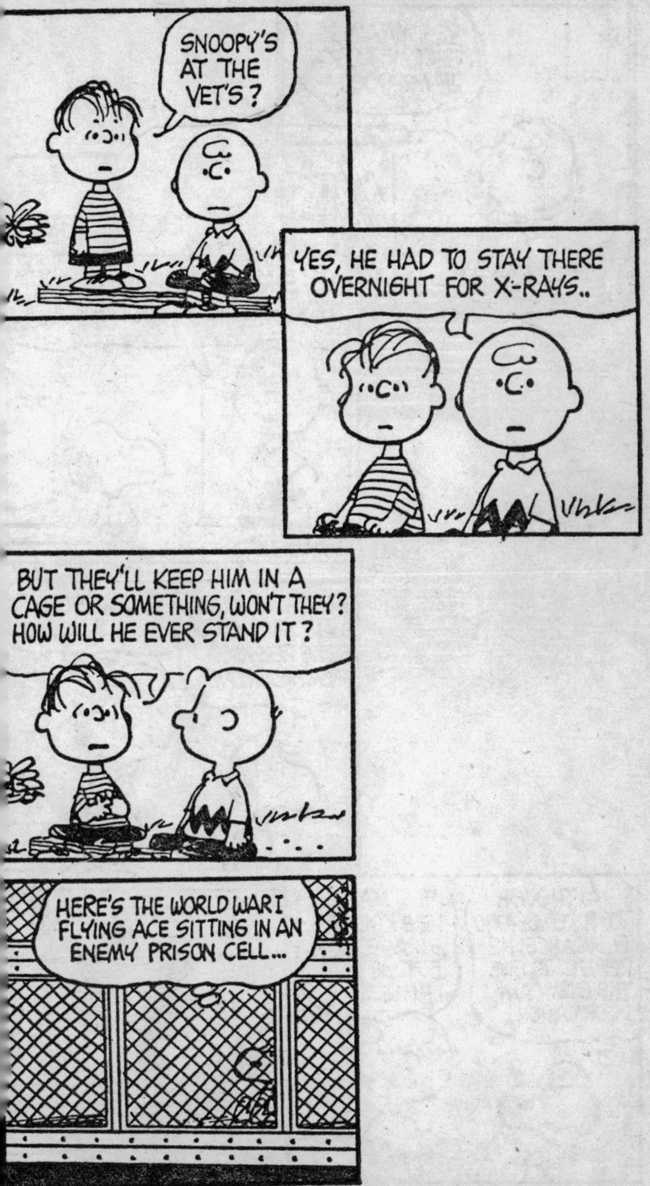
SNOOPY'S AT THE VET'S?
YES, HE HAD TO STAY THERE OVERNIGHT FOR X-RAYS..
BUT THEY'LL KEEP HIM IN A CAGE OR SOMETHING, WON'T THEY? HOW WILL HE EVER STAND IT?
HERE'S THE WORLD WAR I FLYING ACE SITTING IN AN ENEMY PRISON CELL...

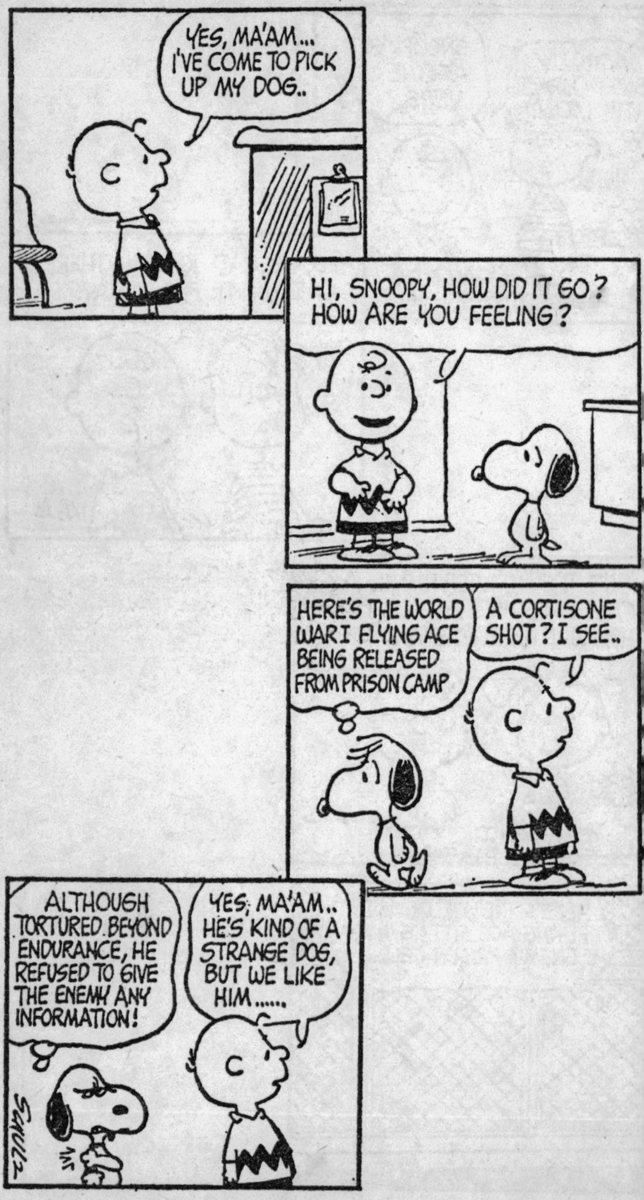
YES, MA'AM... I'VE COME TO PICK UP MY DOG..
HI, SNOOPY, HOW DID IT GO? HOW ARE YOU FEELING?
HERE'S THE WORLD WAR I FLYING ACE BEING RELEASED FROM PRISON CAMP
A CORTISONE SHOT? I SEE..
ALTHOUGH TORTURED BEYOND ENDURANCE, HE REFUSED TO GIVE THE ENEMY ANY INFORMATION!
YES, MA'AM.. HE'S KIND OF A STRANGE DOG, BUT WE LIKE HIM......

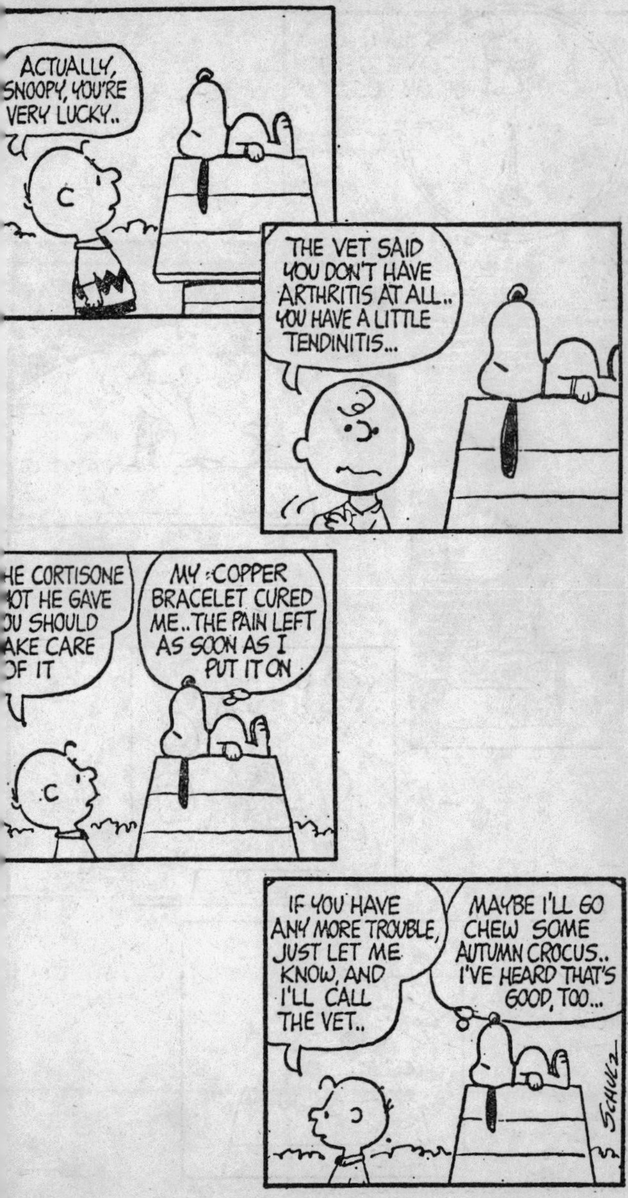
ACTUALLY, SNOOPY, YOU'RE VERY LUCKY..
THE VET SAID YOU DON'T HAVE ARTHRITIS AT ALL.. YOU HAVE A LITTLE TENDINITIS...
HE CORTISONE HOT HE GAVE OU SHOULD AKE CARE OF IT
MY COPPER BRACELET CURED ME..THE PAIN LEFT AS SOON AS I PUT IT ON
IF YOU HAVE ANY MORE TROUBLE, JUST LET ME KNOW, AND I'LL CALL THE VET..
MAYBE I'LL GO CHEW SOME AUTUMN CROCUS.. I'VE HEARD THAT'S GOOD, TOO...
SCHULZ

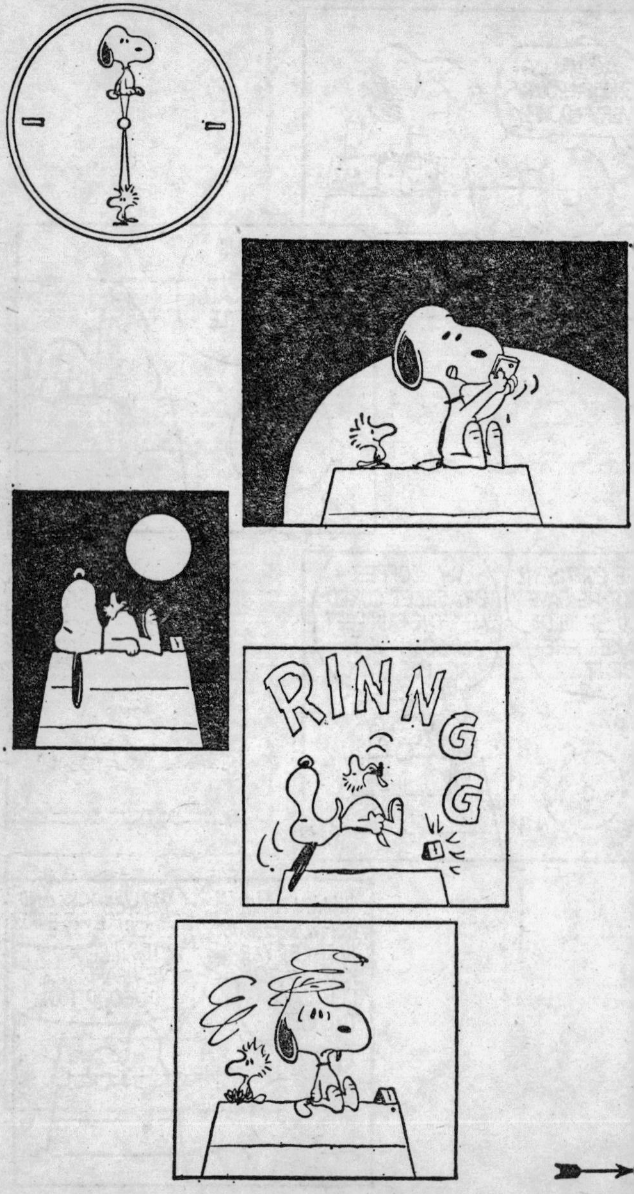
RINNGG

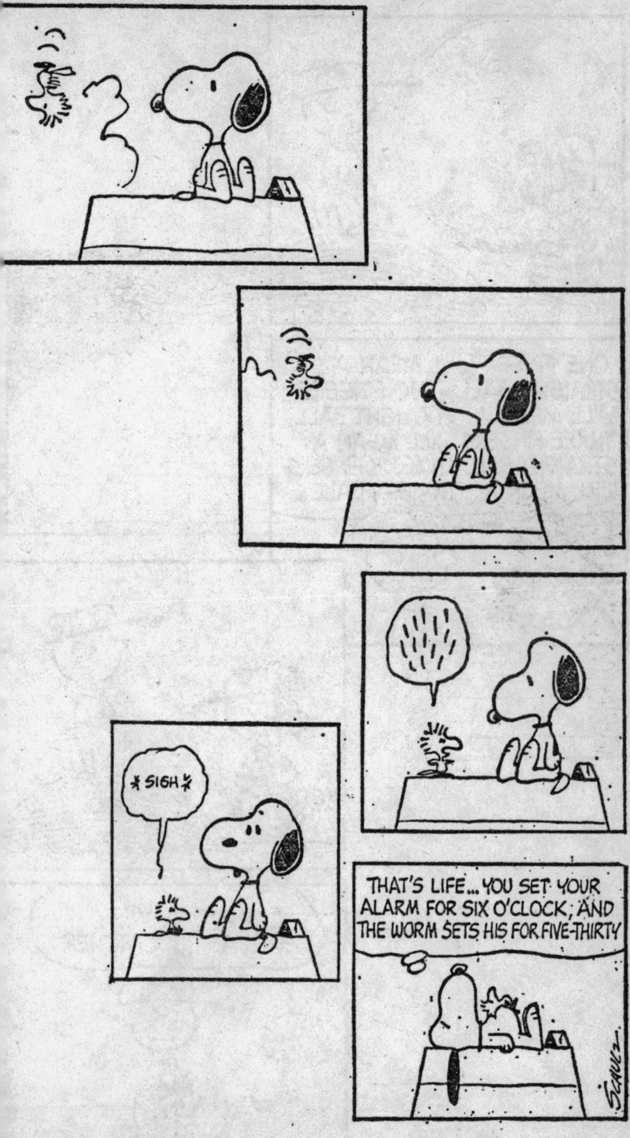
* SIGH *
THAT'S LIFE... YOU SET YOUR ALARM FOR SIX O'CLOCK, AND THE WORM SETS HIS FOR FIVE-THIRTY
SCHULZ

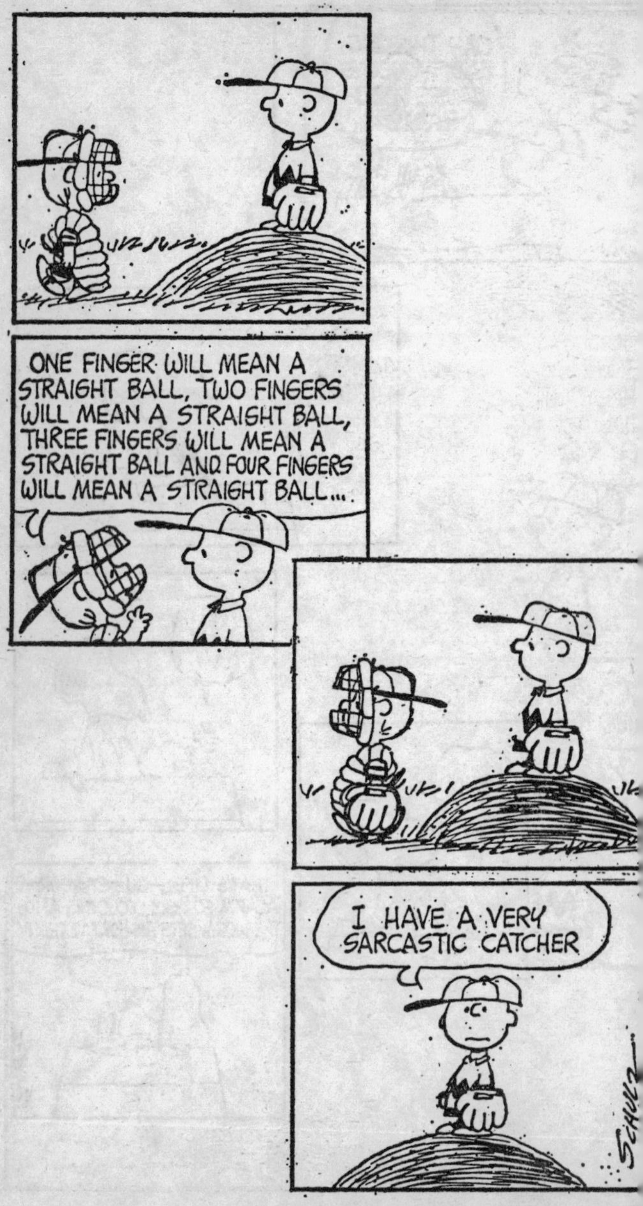
ONE FINGER WILL MEAN A STRAIGHT BALL, TWO FINGERS WILL MEAN A STRAIGHT BALL, THREE FINGERS WILL MEAN A STRAIGHT BALL AND FOUR FINGERS WILL MEAN A STRAIGHT BALL...
I HAVE A VERY SARCASTIC CATCHER
SCHULZ

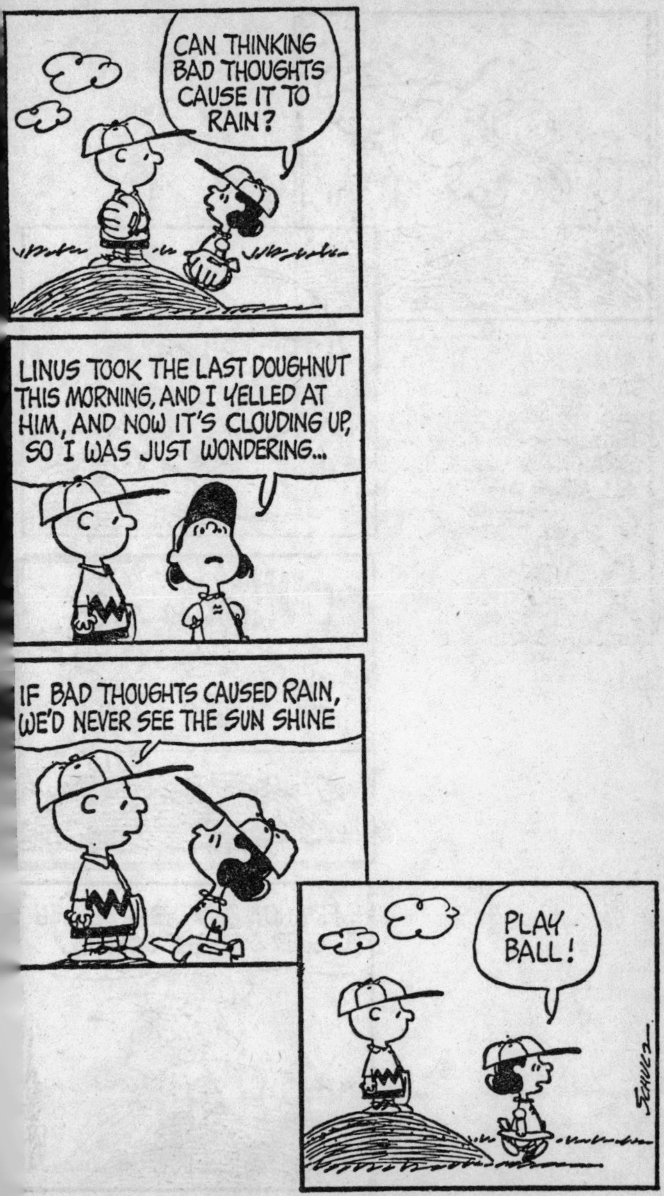
CAN THINKING BAD THOUGHTS CAUSE IT TO RAIN?
LINUS TOOK THE LAST DOUGHNUT THIS MORNING, AND I YELLED AT HIM, AND NOW IT'S CLOUDING UP, SO I WAS JUST WONDERING...
IF BAD THOUGHTS CAUSED RAIN, WE'D NEVER SEE THE SUN SHINE
PLAY BALL!
SCHULZ

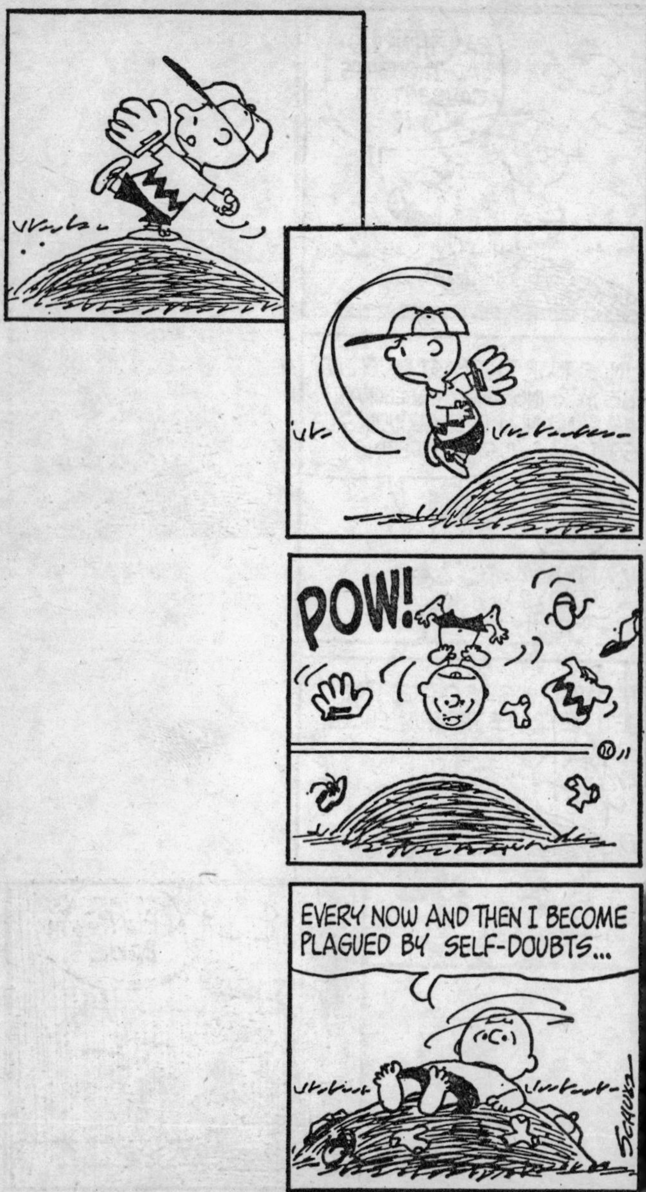
POW!
EVERY NOW AND THEN I BECOME PLAGUED BY SELF-DOUBTS...

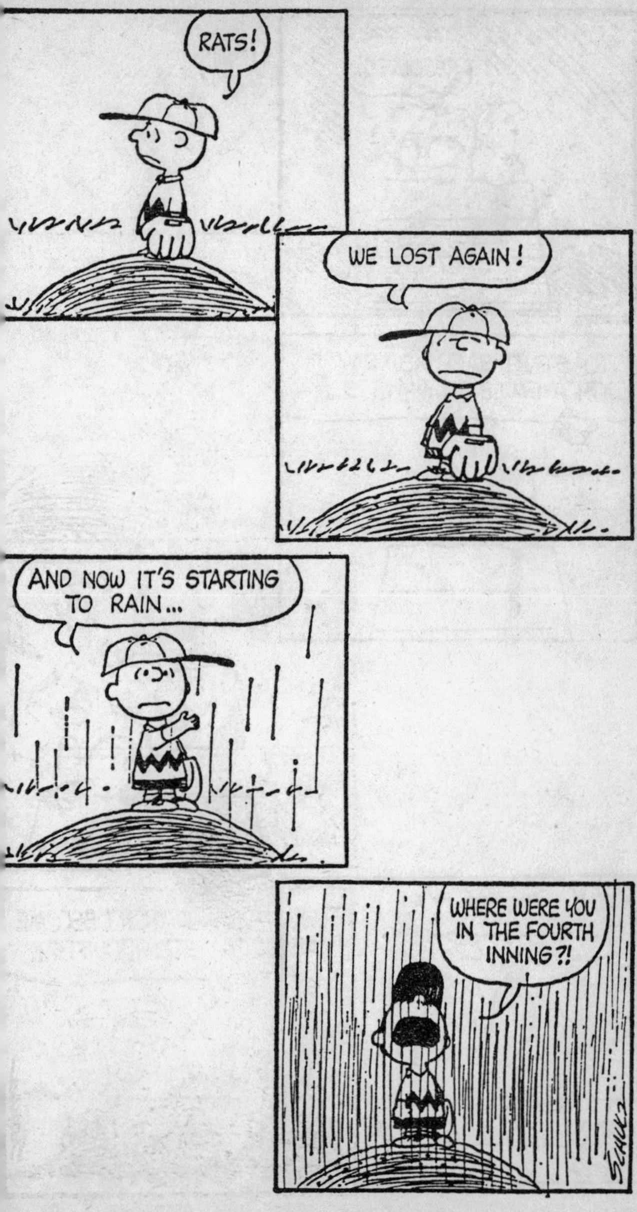
RATS!
WE LOST AGAIN!
AND NOW IT'S STARTING TO RAIN...
WHERE WERE YOU IN THE FOURTH INNING?!
SCHULZ

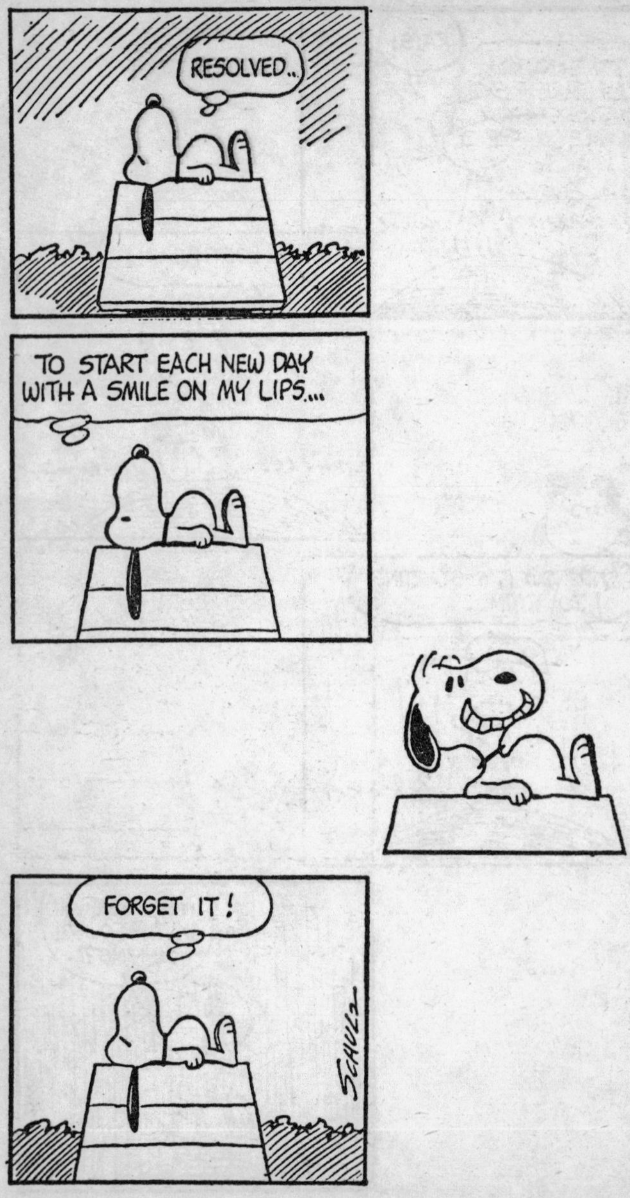
RESOLVED..
TO START EACH NEW DAY WITH A SMILE ON MY LIPS....
FORGET IT!

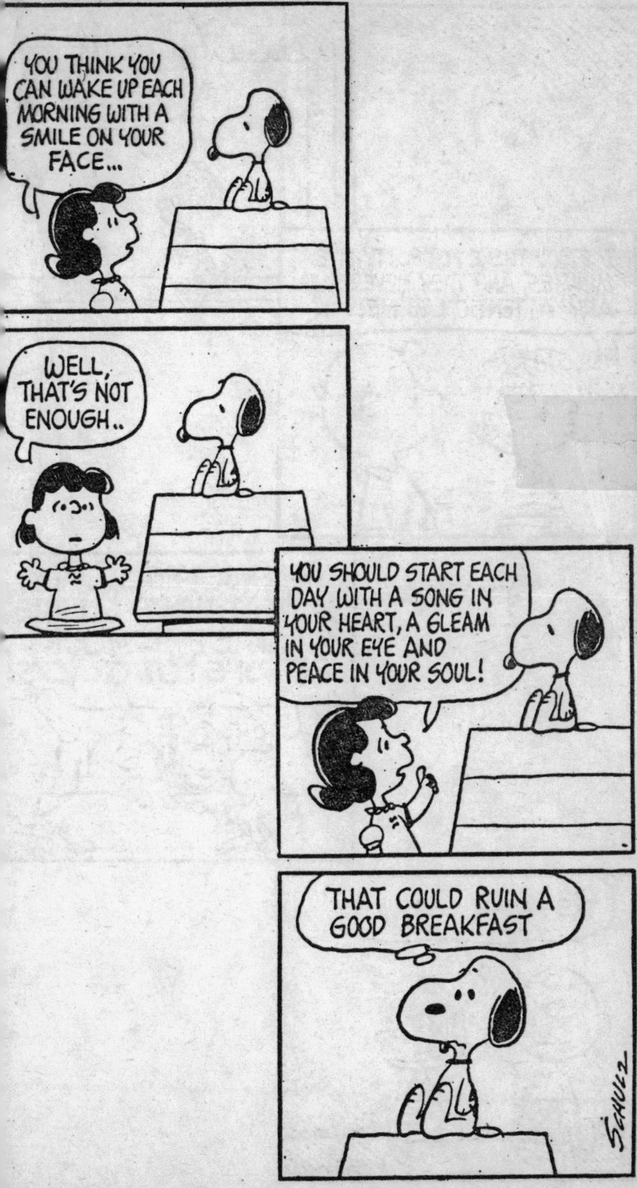
YOU THINK YOU CAN WAKE UP EACH MORNING WITH A SMILE ON YOUR FACE...
WELL, THAT'S NOT ENOUGH..
YOU SHOULD START EACH DAY WITH A SONG IN YOUR HEART, A GLEAM IN YOUR EYE AND PEACE IN YOUR SOUL!
THAT COULD RUIN A GOOD BREAKFAST
SCHULZ

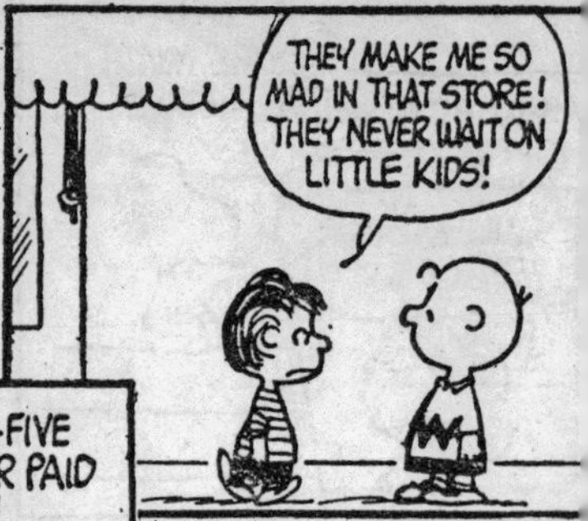
THEY MAKE ME SO MAD IN THAT STORE! THEY NEVER WAIT ON LITTLE KIDS!

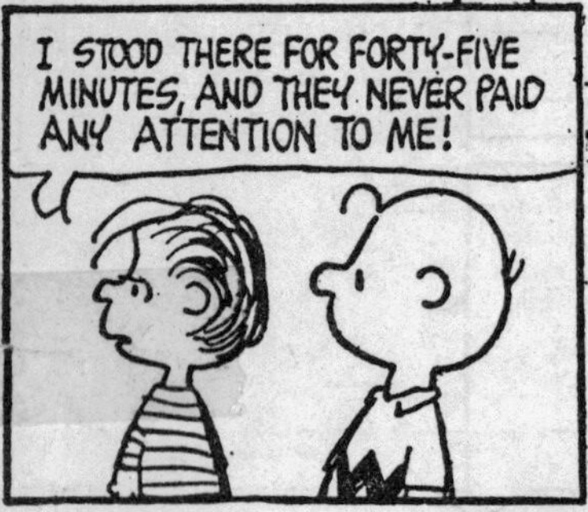
I STOOD THERE FOR FORTY-FIVE MINUTES, AND THEY NEVER PAID ANY ATTENTION TO ME!

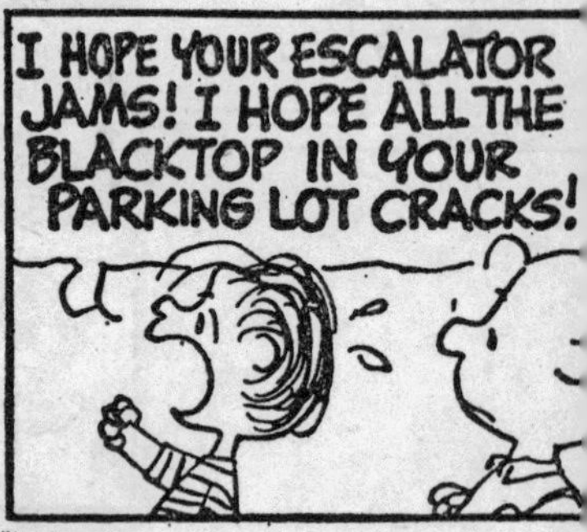
I HOPE YOUR ESCALATOR JAMS! I HOPE ALL THE BLACKTOP IN YOUR PARKING LOT CRACKS!

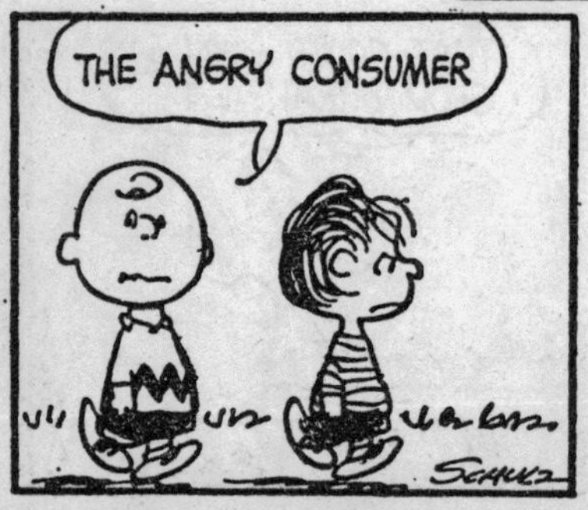
THE ANGRY CONSUMER
SCHULZ

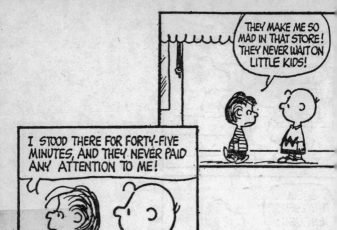

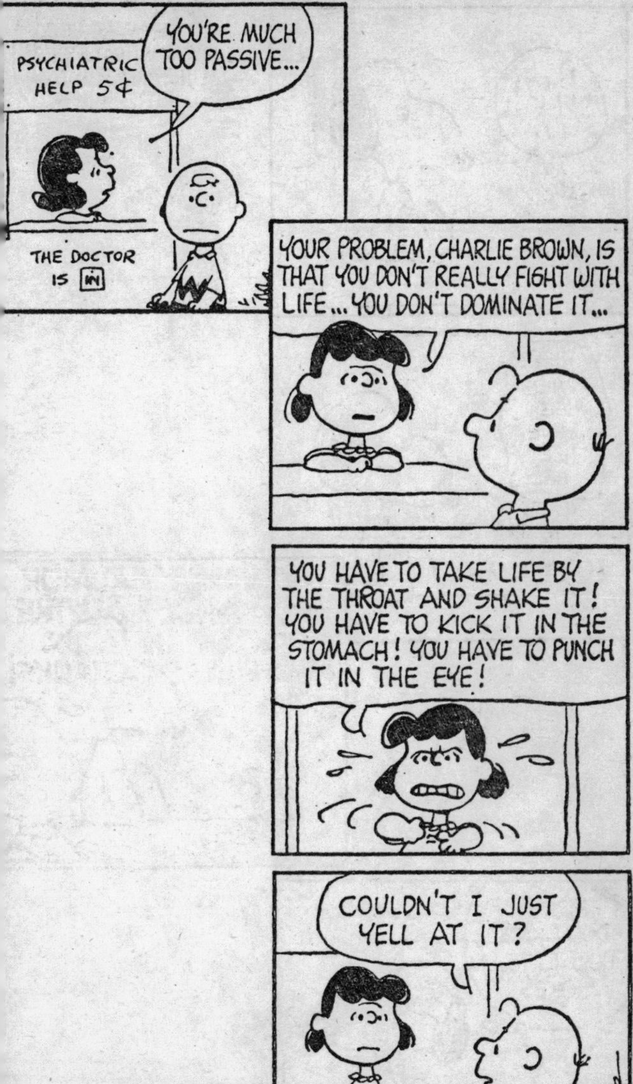
PSYCHIATRIC HELP 5¢
YOU'RE MUCH TOO PASSIVE...
THE DOCTOR IS IN
YOUR PROBLEM, CHARLIE BROWN, IS THAT YOU DON'T REALLY FIGHT WITH LIFE... YOU DON'T DOMINATE IT...
YOU HAVE TO TAKE LIFE BY THE THROAT AND SHAKE IT! YOU HAVE TO KICK IT IN THE STOMACH! YOU HAVE TO PUNCH IT IN THE EYE!
COULDN'T I JUST YELL AT IT?
THE DOCTOR IS IN
SCHULZ

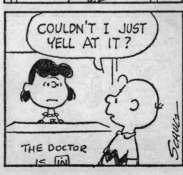

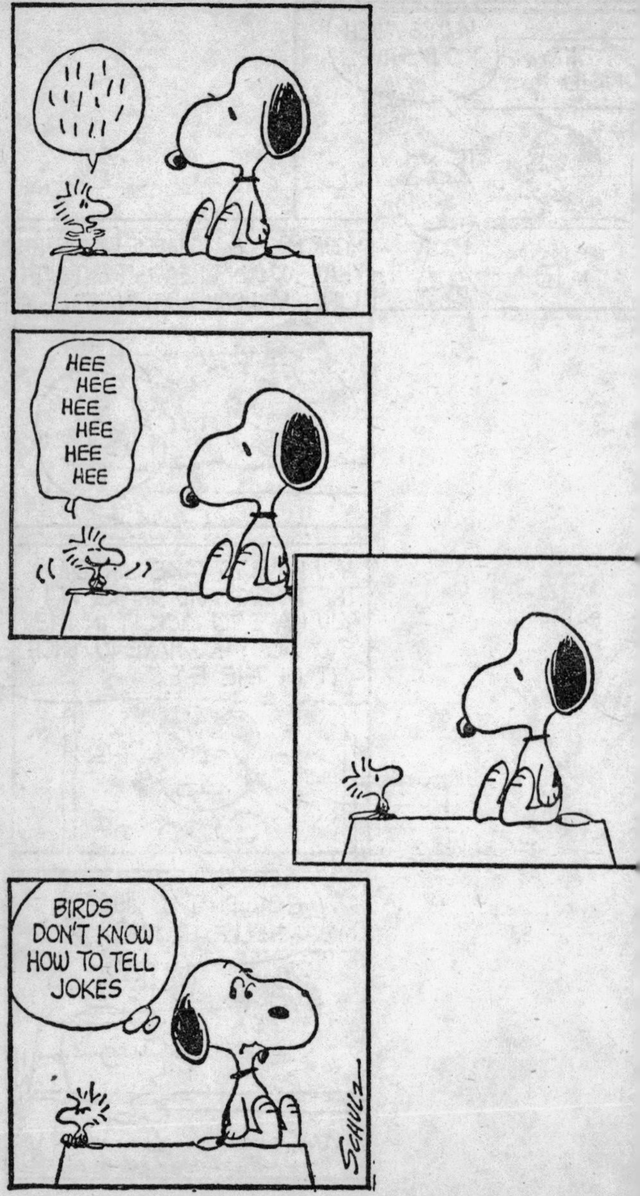
HEE HEE HEE HEE HEE HEE
BIRDS DON'T KNOW HOW TO TELL JOKES
SCHULZ

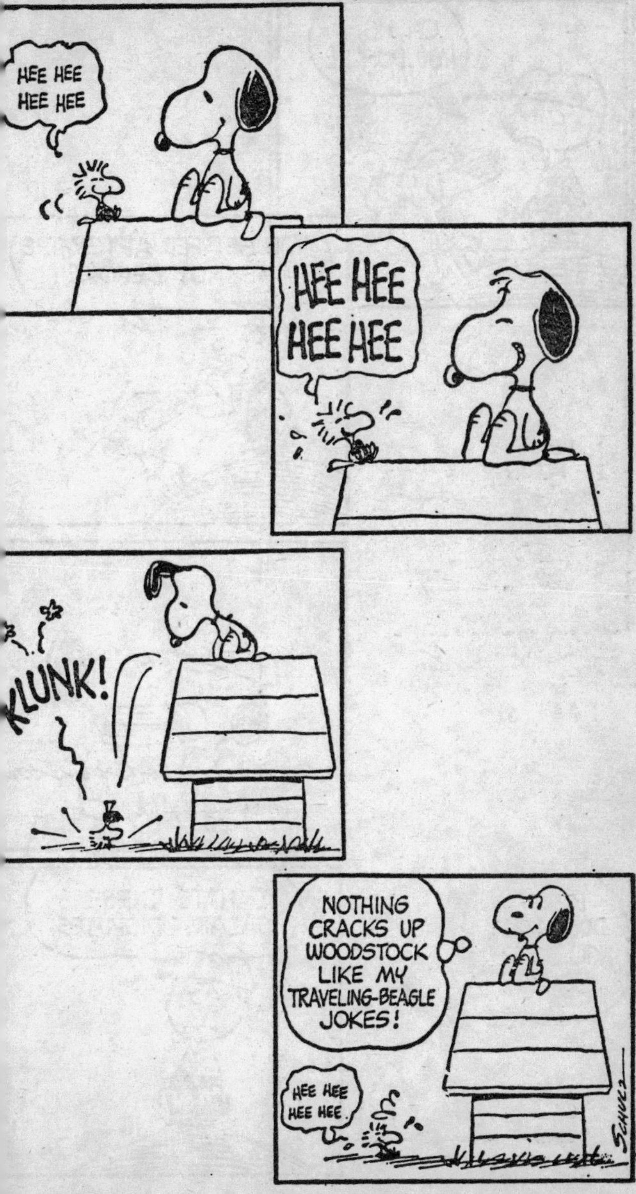
HEE HEE HEE HEE
HEE HEE HEE HEE
KLUNK!
NOTHING CRACKS UP WOODSTOCK LIKE MY TRAVELING-BEAGLE JOKES!
HEE HEE HEE HEE
SCHULZ

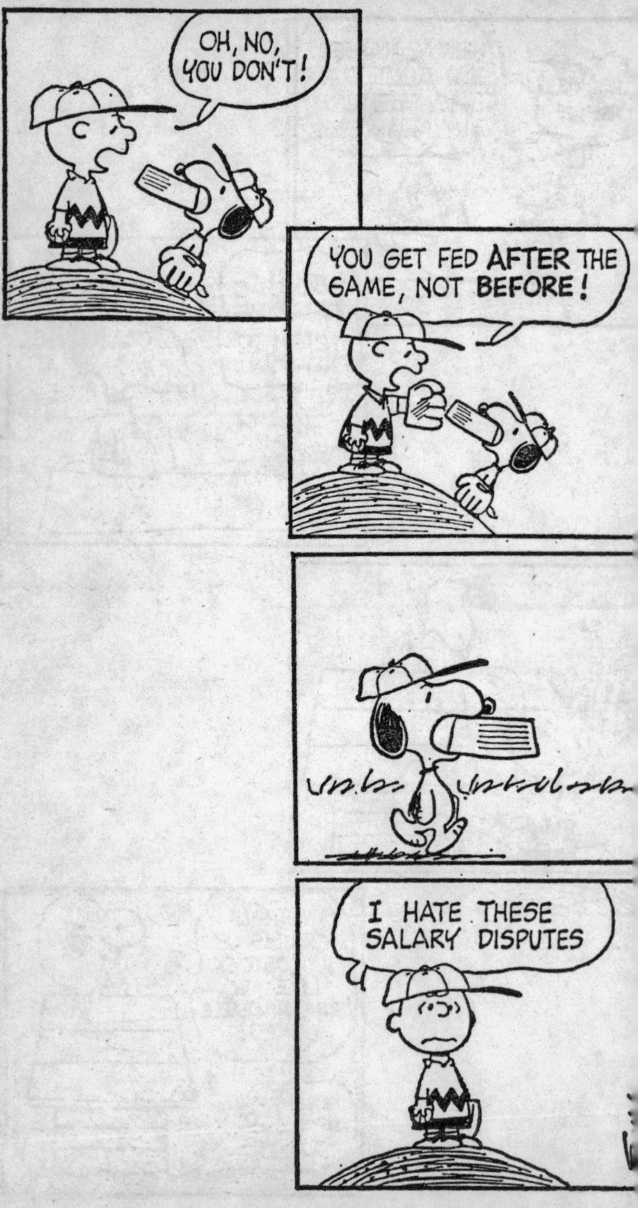
OH, NO, YOU DON'T!
YOU GET FED **AFTER** THE GAME, NOT **BEFORE**!
I HATE THESE SALARY DISPUTES

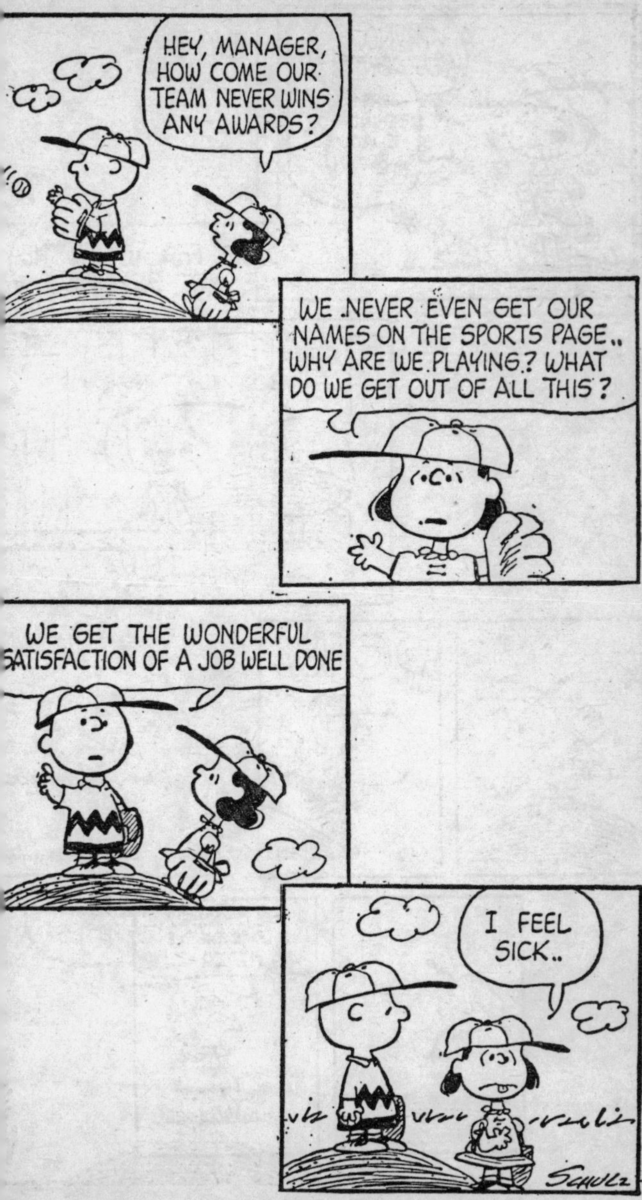
HEY, MANAGER, HOW COME OUR TEAM NEVER WINS ANY AWARDS?
WE NEVER EVEN GET OUR NAMES ON THE SPORTS PAGE.. WHY ARE WE PLAYING? WHAT DO WE GET OUT OF ALL THIS?
WE GET THE WONDERFUL SATISFACTION OF A JOB WELL DONE
I FEEL SICK..
SCHULZ

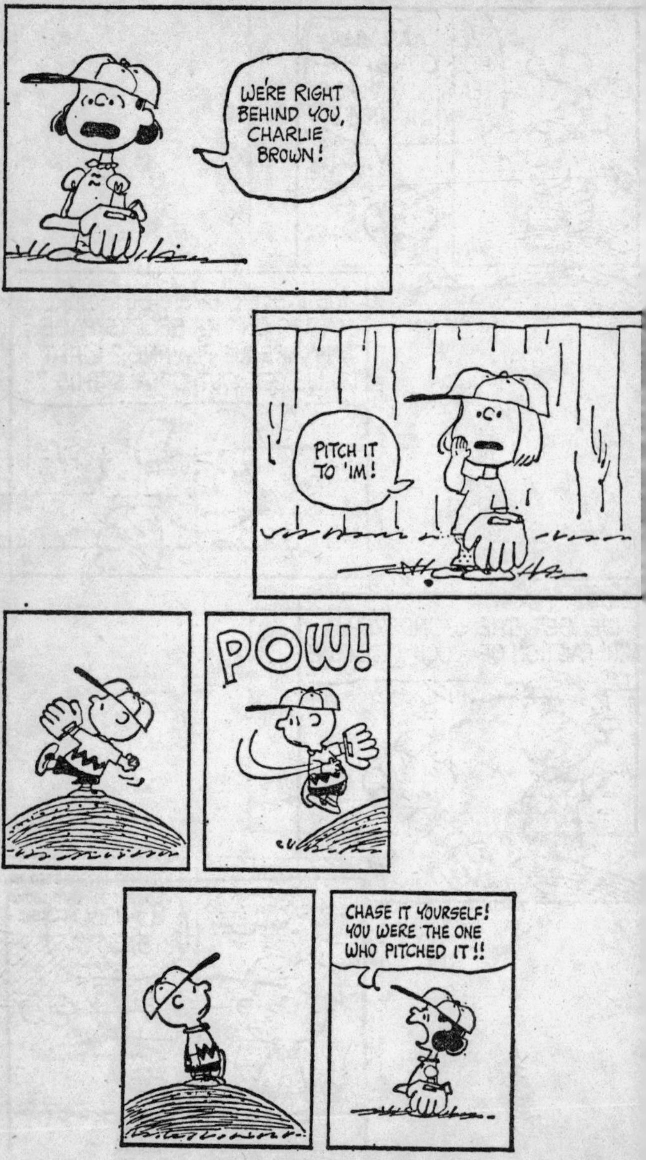
WE'RE RIGHT BEHIND YOU, CHARLIE BROWN!
PITCH IT TO 'IM!
POW!
CHASE IT YOURSELF! YOU WERE THE ONE WHO PITCHED IT!!

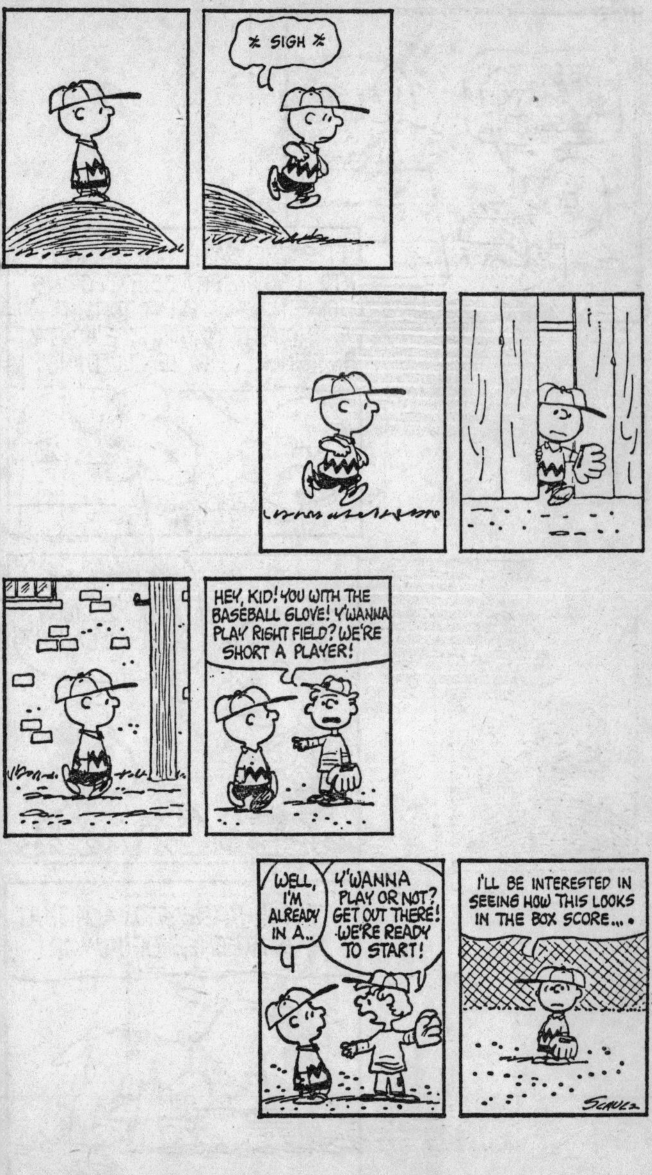
* SIGH *
HEY, KID! YOU WITH THE BASEBALL GLOVE! Y'WANNA PLAY RIGHT FIELD? WE'RE SHORT A PLAYER!
WELL, I'M ALREADY IN A..
Y'WANNA PLAY OR NOT? GET OUT THERE! WE'RE READY TO START!
I'LL BE INTERESTED IN SEEING HOW THIS LOOKS IN THE BOX SCORE....
SCHULZ

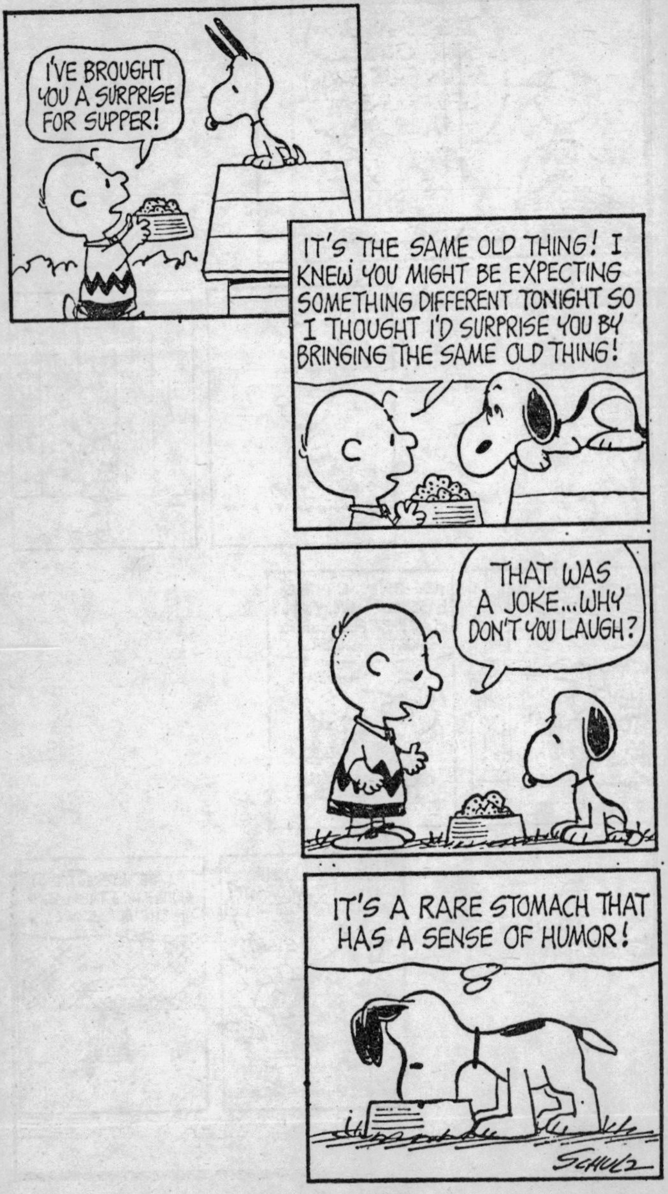
I'VE BROUGHT YOU A SURPRISE FOR SUPPER!
IT'S THE SAME OLD THING! I KNEW YOU MIGHT BE EXPECTING SOMETHING DIFFERENT TONIGHT SO I THOUGHT I'D SURPRISE YOU BY BRINGING THE SAME OLD THING!
THAT WAS A JOKE...WHY DON'T YOU LAUGH?
IT'S A RARE STOMACH THAT HAS A SENSE OF HUMOR!
SCHULZ

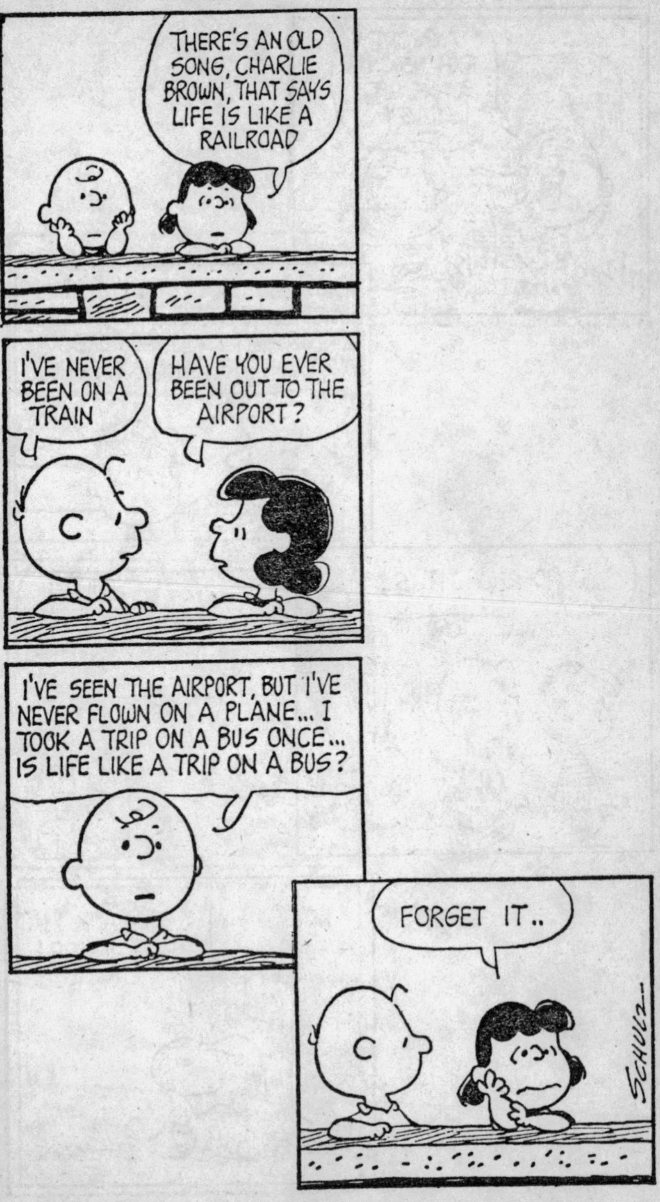
THERE'S AN OLD SONG, CHARLIE BROWN, THAT SAYS LIFE IS LIKE A RAILROAD
I'VE NEVER BEEN ON A TRAIN
HAVE YOU EVER BEEN OUT TO THE AIRPORT?
I'VE SEEN THE AIRPORT, BUT I'VE NEVER FLOWN ON A PLANE... I TOOK A TRIP ON A BUS ONCE... IS LIFE LIKE A TRIP ON A BUS?
FORGET IT..
SCHULZ

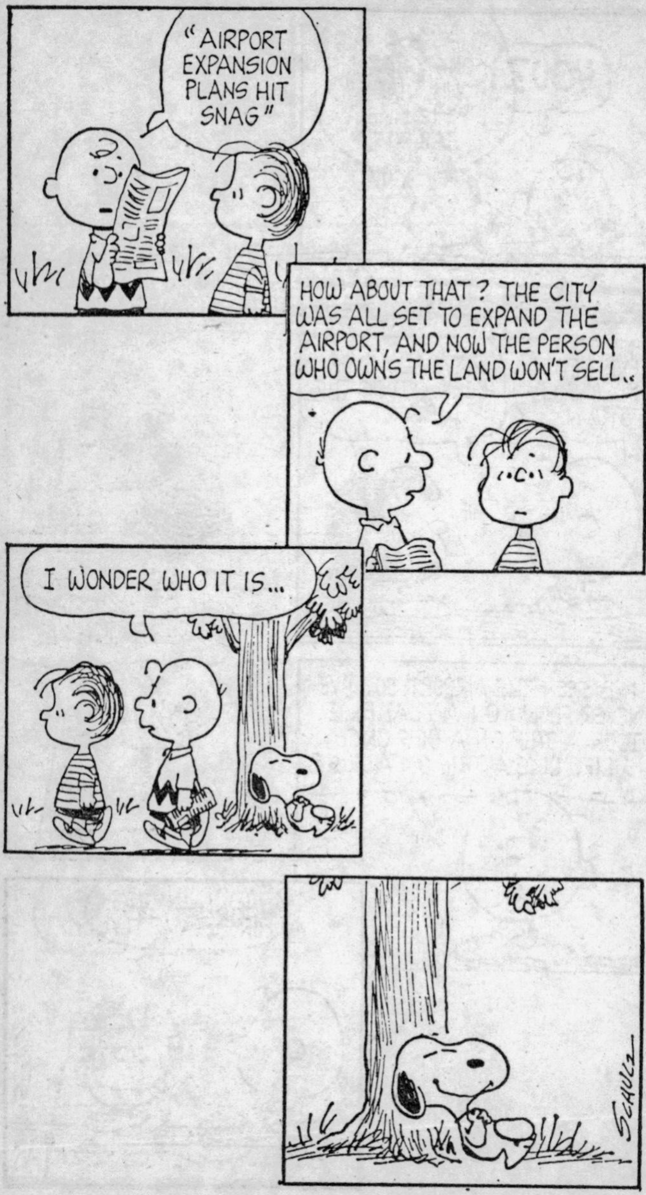
"AIRPORT EXPANSION PLANS HIT SNAG"
HOW ABOUT THAT? THE CITY WAS ALL SET TO EXPAND THE AIRPORT, AND NOW THE PERSON WHO OWNS THE LAND WON'T SELL..
I WONDER WHO IT IS...
SCHULZ

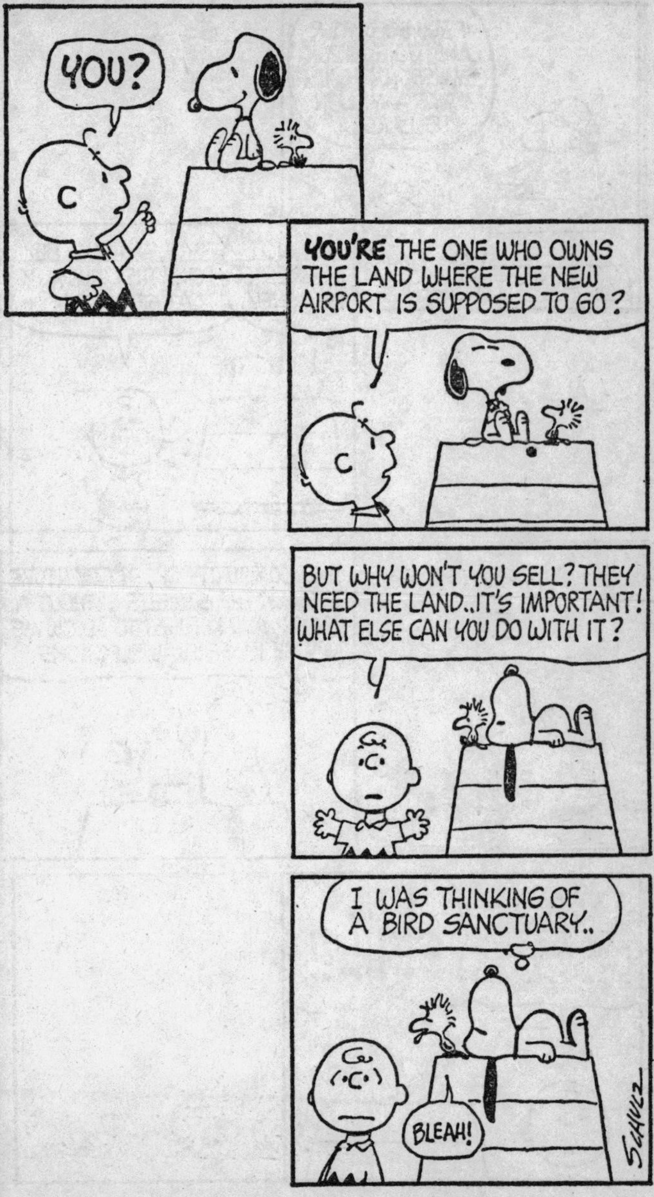
YOU?
YOU'RE THE ONE WHO OWNS THE LAND WHERE THE NEW AIRPORT IS SUPPOSED TO GO?
BUT WHY WON'T YOU SELL? THEY NEED THE LAND..IT'S IMPORTANT! WHAT ELSE CAN YOU DO WITH IT?
I WAS THINKING OF A BIRD SANCTUARY..
BLEAH!
SCHULZ

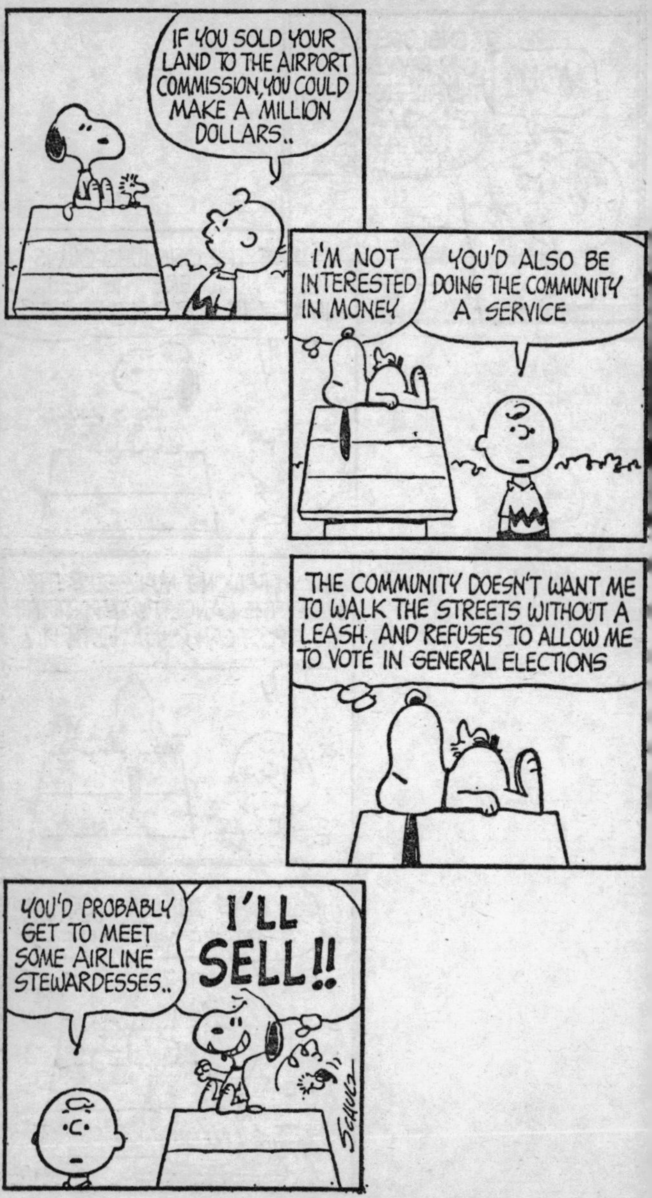
IF YOU SOLD YOUR LAND TO THE AIRPORT COMMISSION, YOU COULD MAKE A MILLION DOLLARS..
I'M NOT INTERESTED IN MONEY
YOU'D ALSO BE DOING THE COMMUNITY A SERVICE
THE COMMUNITY DOESN'T WANT ME TO WALK THE STREETS WITHOUT A LEASH, AND REFUSES TO ALLOW ME TO VOTE IN GENERAL ELECTIONS
YOU'D PROBABLY GET TO MEET SOME AIRLINE STEWARDESSES..
I'LL SELL!!
SCHULZ

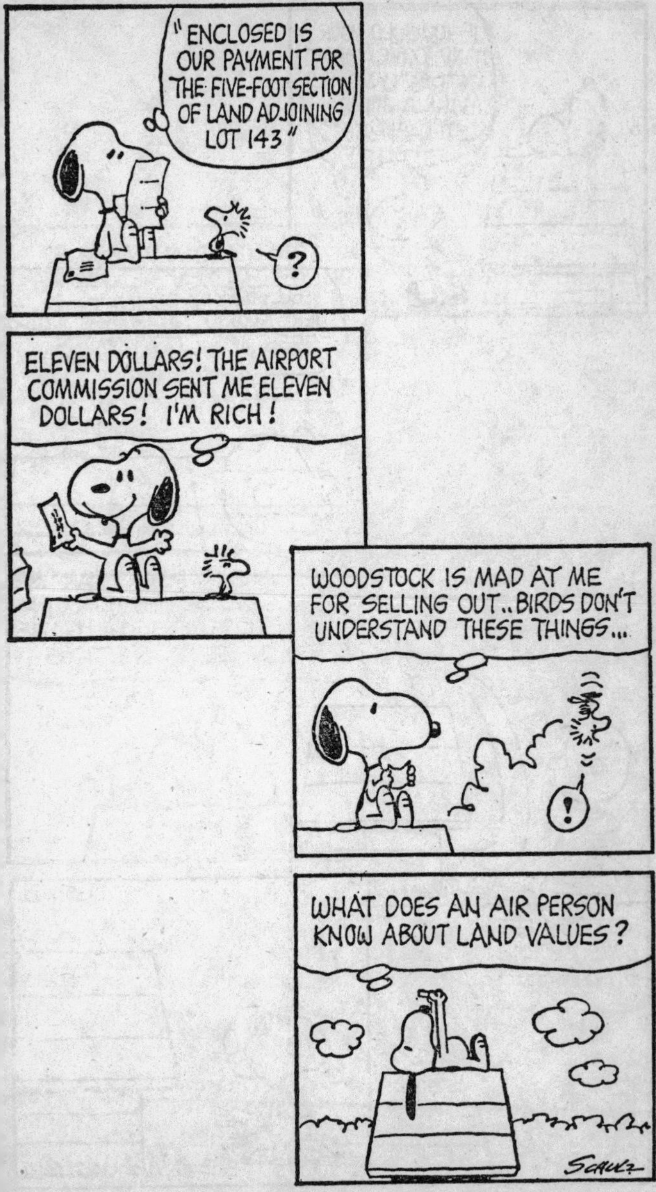
"ENCLOSED IS OUR PAYMENT FOR THE FIVE-FOOT SECTION OF LAND ADJOINING LOT 143"
?
ELEVEN DOLLARS! THE AIRPORT COMMISSION SENT ME ELEVEN DOLLARS! I'M RICH!
WOODSTOCK IS MAD AT ME FOR SELLING OUT.. BIRDS DON'T UNDERSTAND THESE THINGS...
!
WHAT DOES AN AIR PERSON KNOW ABOUT LAND VALUES?
SCHULZ

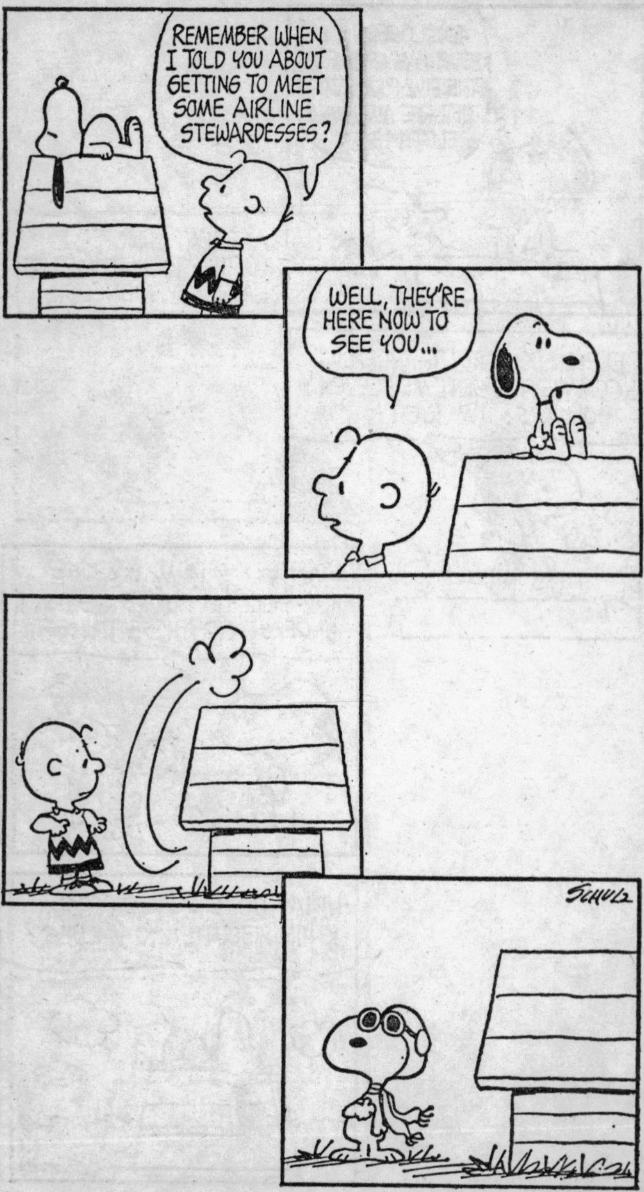
REMEMBER WHEN I TOLD YOU ABOUT GETTING TO MEET SOME AIRLINE STEWARDESSES?
WELL, THEY'RE HERE NOW TO SEE YOU...
SCHULZ

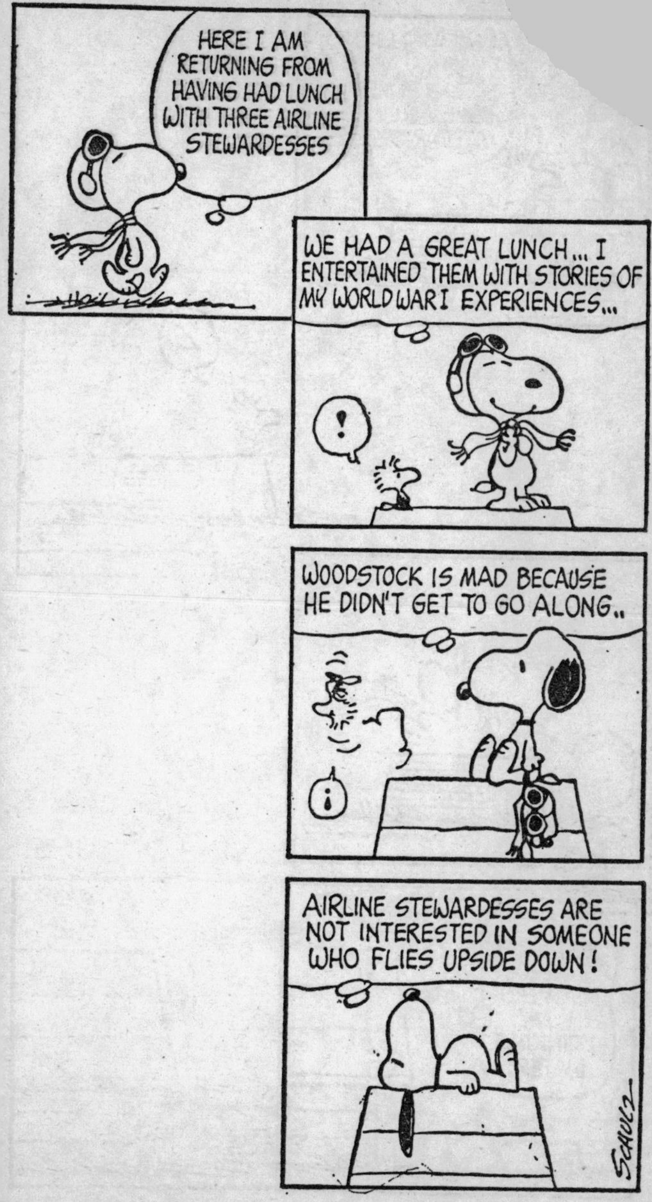
HERE I AM RETURNING FROM HAVING HAD LUNCH WITH THREE AIRLINE STEWARDESSES
WE HAD A GREAT LUNCH... I ENTERTAINED THEM WITH STORIES OF MY WORLD WAR I EXPERIENCES...
!
WOODSTOCK IS MAD BECAUSE HE DIDN'T GET TO GO ALONG..
¡
AIRLINE STEWARDESSES ARE NOT INTERESTED IN SOMEONE WHO FLIES UPSIDE DOWN!
SCHULZ

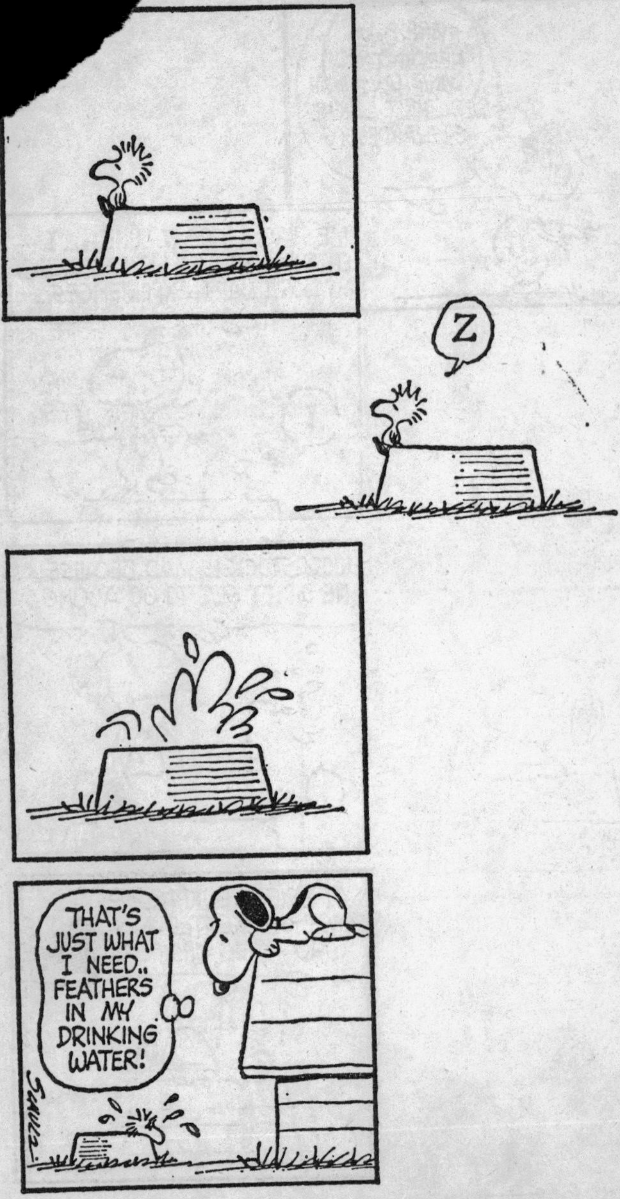
Z
THAT'S JUST WHAT I NEED.. FEATHERS IN MY DRINKING WATER!
SCHULZ

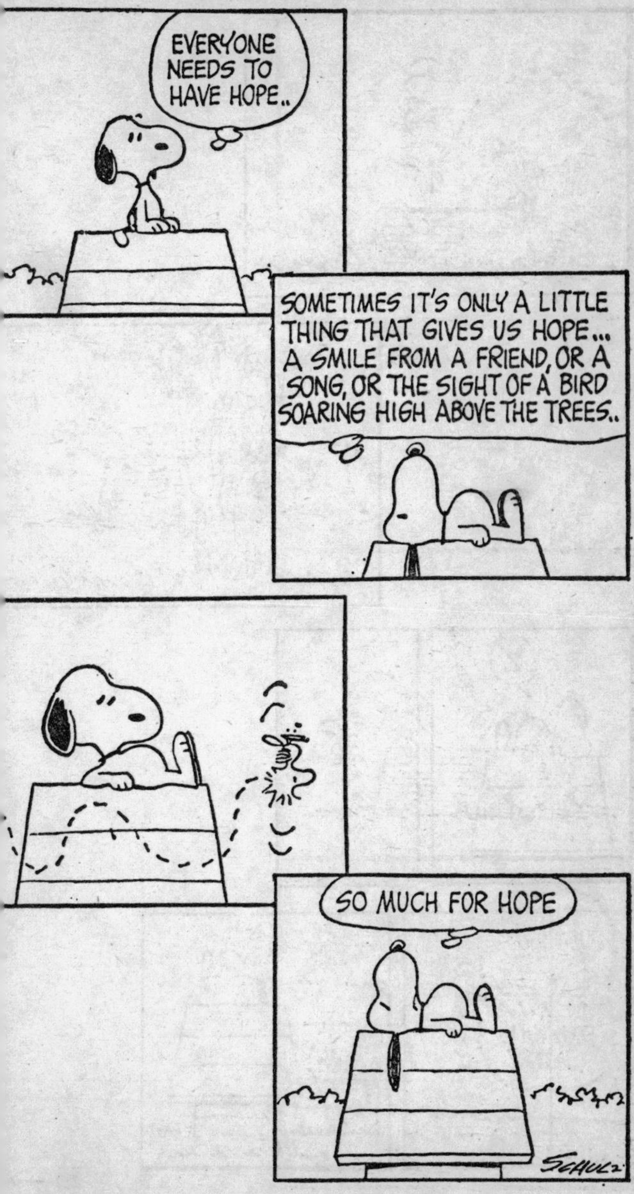
EVERYONE NEEDS TO HAVE HOPE..
SOMETIMES IT'S ONLY A LITTLE THING THAT GIVES US HOPE... A SMILE FROM A FRIEND, OR A SONG, OR THE SIGHT OF A BIRD SOARING HIGH ABOVE THE TREES..
SO MUCH FOR HOPE
SCHULZ

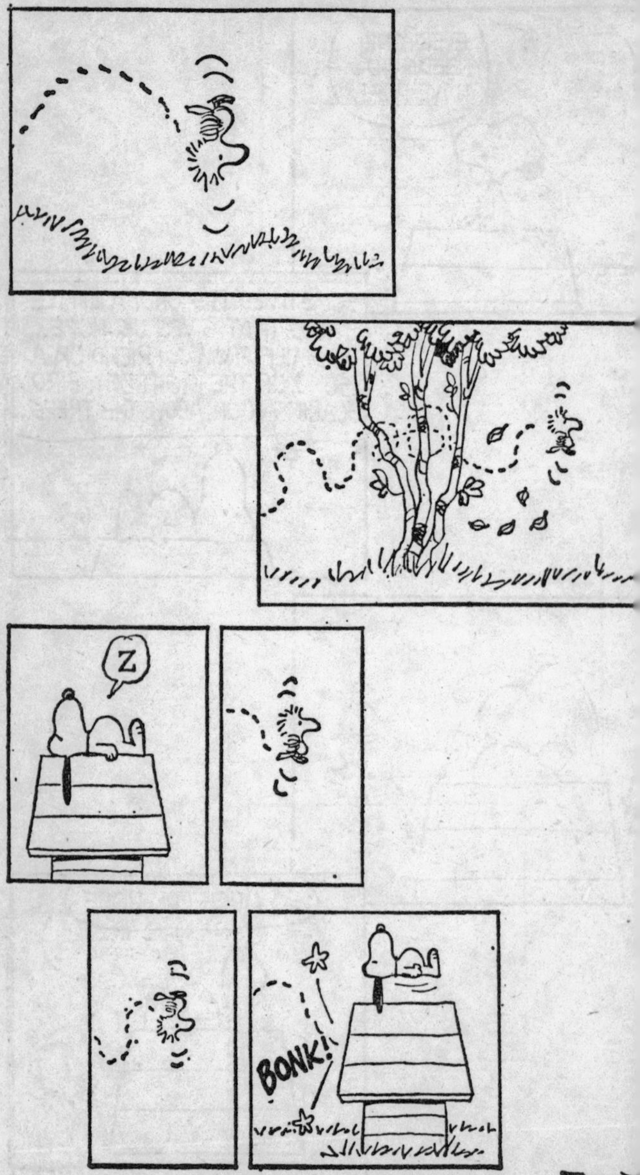
Z
BONK!

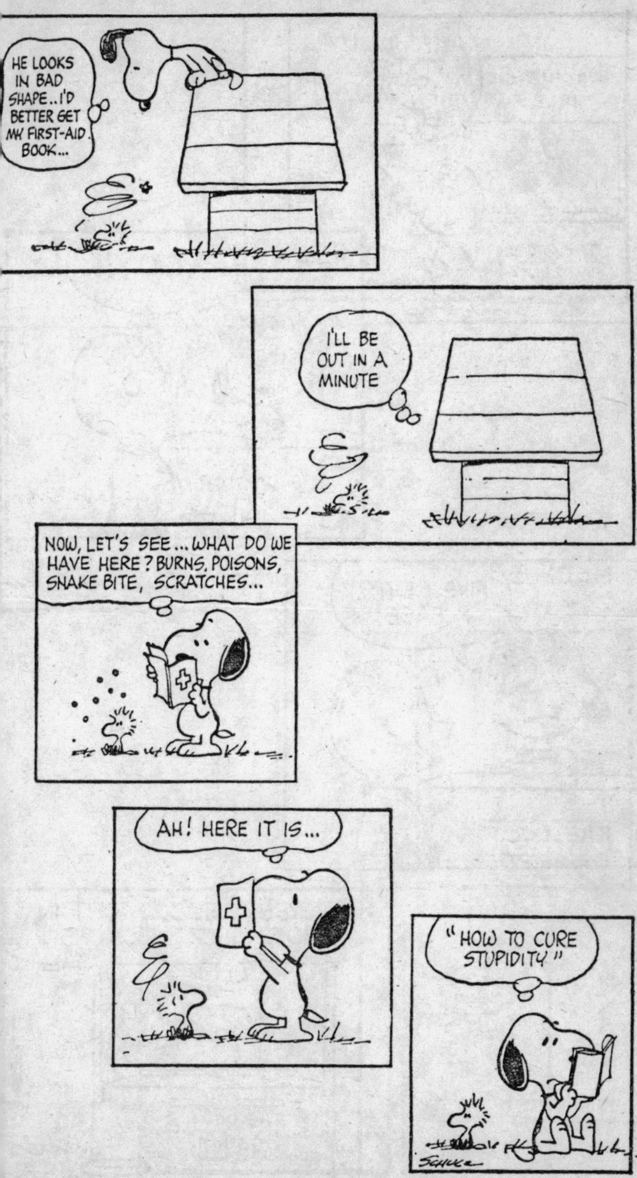
HE LOOKS IN BAD SHAPE..I'D BETTER GET MY FIRST-AID BOOK...
I'LL BE OUT IN A MINUTE
NOW, LET'S SEE...WHAT DO WE HAVE HERE? BURNS, POISONS, SNAKE BITE, SCRATCHES...
AH! HERE IT IS...
"HOW TO CURE STUPIDITY"

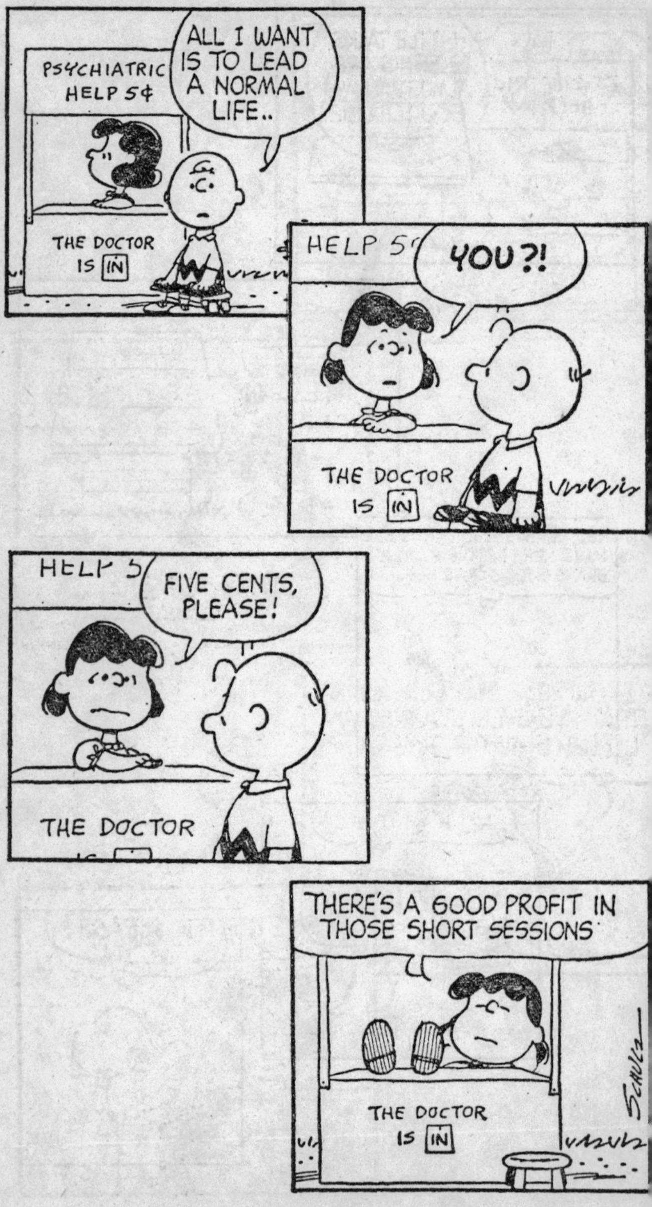
PSYCHIATRIC HELP 5¢
ALL I WANT IS TO LEAD A NORMAL LIFE..
THE DOCTOR IS IN
YOU?!
THE DOCTOR IS IN
FIVE CENTS, PLEASE!
THE DOCTOR
THERE'S A GOOD PROFIT IN THOSE SHORT SESSIONS
THE DOCTOR IS IN
SCHULZ

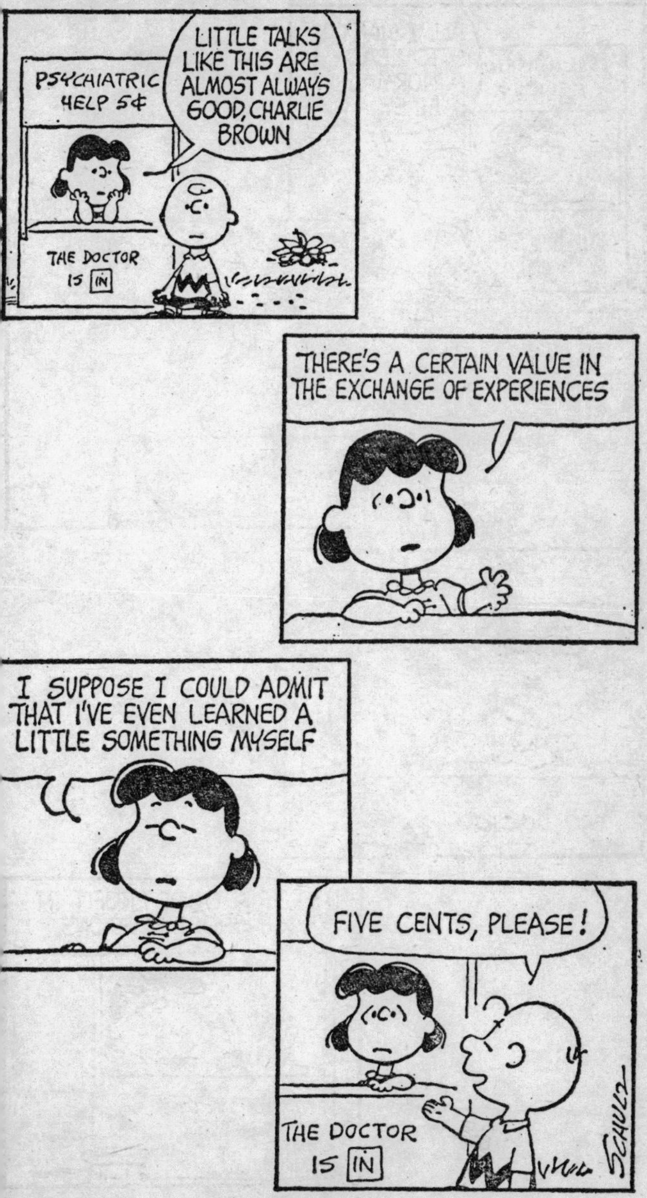
PSYCHIATRIC HELP 5¢
LITTLE TALKS LIKE THIS ARE ALMOST ALWAYS GOOD, CHARLIE BROWN
THE DOCTOR IS IN
THERE'S A CERTAIN VALUE IN THE EXCHANGE OF EXPERIENCES
I SUPPOSE I COULD ADMIT THAT I'VE EVEN LEARNED A LITTLE SOMETHING MYSELF
FIVE CENTS, PLEASE!
THE DOCTOR IS IN
SCHULZ